History of the Future

HISTORY OF THE FUTURE

▼

MICHAEL KESSLER

Writers Club Press
San Jose New York Lincoln Shanghai

History of the Future

Writers Club Press
an imprint of iUniverse, Inc.

For information address:
iUniverse, Inc.
5220 S. 16th St., Suite 200
Lincoln, NE 68512
www.iuniverse.com

Michael Kessler
P.O. Box 21546
Louisville, KY
40221-0546
502-375-0340

ISBN: 0-595-22225-0

Printed in the United States of America

CONTENTS

"If you are thinking

A year ahead, sow seed.

If you are thinking ten years ahead

Plant a tree.

If you are thinking one hundred years ahead

Educate the people.

By sowing seed once,

You will harvest once.

By planting a tree,

You will harvest tenfold.

By educating the people,

You will harvest one hundred-fold."

Anonymous Chinese poet
2,500 years ago

INTRODUCTION

In the middle of the 1970s, I taught high school in Louisville, Kentucky. The social studies department decided to offer a course based on Alvin Toffler's book, *Future Shock*. Since I was the only one of two in my department who had even read the book and was the only one willing to teach the course, I got the job. The class was a big hit with the students and opened the door to a whole new life for me.

Over the next few years, I was introduced more and more to the dangers facing our planet and the exciting solutions to meet them. So I left the classroom and decided to create ways to broaden and deepen this body of knowledge, with all of its opportunities, among the general population of the world.

Running parallel with these events was my introduction to music. I had helped to form a musical group that achieved some local recognition. By the effect the group had on audiences, I concluded that music was *the* medium to reach large numbers of people in a meaningful way.

Leaving my teaching career, I moved to Nashville to launch my musical one. Although my stay there did not produce the breakthroughs I wanted, it did give me freedom to write songs and to expand my research. From Toffler's work I was quickly led to the works of Albert Einstein and R. Buckminster Fuller.

Before Einstein, the world operated on the basis of a pool of traditions that made up our picture of reality. Fuller's work revealed that the truths of these traditions are outdated in light of the information explosion sparked by Einstein. Like other centuries before us, the twentieth century has become a time of transition from one *way of thinking* to another. The purpose of this book is to assist the reader in understanding the nature of this transition and to make clear the importance of the individual's role in its successful outcome.

Fuller spent over 50 years of his life developing a technology based upon Einstein's science. He concluded that if we used the principles of the real universe in the design of our technology, we can create a wealthy, global society that lives in peace with the environment rather than at the present expense of it.

After moving back to Louisville, I created a second avenue to popularize this information. *History of the Future* is a lecture/workshop using dialogue and slides. The program covers the Einstein/Fuller reality shift and its impact on four major traditions: physics, biology, economics, and politics. I use these four to serve as the foundations of what we call reality.

After years of performing my music and presenting the lecture around the United States, in Europe, and Russia, I took the advice of many people to put it all in a book: a book written in simple language to show it is now time to create one nation from the "countries" of Earth.

Today all "countries" are faced with dangers that exceed our national level of thinking. What we are up against, especially in regard to the environment, threatens us as *living beings* on the planet. Continued loyalty to these old ideas of reality have created problems that truly can end all life on Earth.

If we are facing global threats, then it only makes common sense to create a global means to deal with them. What is needed, according to Einstein, Fuller, and a host of others, is the creation of a constitutional world government, a *global* nation.

Some say the United Nations is already here to deal with global questions. However, the United Nations is not able to do that adequately. In 1783, the new American nation created a system of government just like the United Nations to meet its problems. The central flaw to this kind of government is that it has no *power* to govern. Each member state keeps its individual freedom from the system. Each state decides whether or not it will obey the decisions of the Congress. The government does not have the power to rule by *law*.

The same situation exists with the United Nations. Each "country" has the power to obey or ignore what the United Nations decides. With the United Nations, as with the 1783 American form of government, each member is more powerful than the central government, unless the government acts with *unified* power.

In 1787, the American nation decided it had to have a government with unified power if the nation was to survive. The separate states, like the "countries" of Europe, were beginning to have disagreements that threatened to break out into open warfare. The founders of the 1783 American system re-met in Philadelphia to come up with another system of government.

They quickly concluded that their only hope of solving national problems was to create a national government to rule the "country" by law. They wrote the Constitution to give the new national government legal authority to meet the problems of the whole nation. Its opening lines say it all: "We, the people, in order to create a more perfect Union…"

Today the situation is the same, except now the problems are global. Like the young American nation of 1787, we, as citizens of the world, are beset by problems involving us all but we have no true government to deal with them. What is needed now is the creation of a real world government to meet real world problems.

Throughout the text of this book the word "country" is in quotation marks. As you will see, the bottom-line message of this book is that there are no "countries." When you view our planet from a distance, there are no little dotted lines on the surface with a "country" on one side and a foreign "country" on the other. There is only our little planet in the vastness of space. We do not live in "countries"; rather, the concept lives on in us as outdated traditions.

During the period when all of these "countries" were created, someone came up with the word *patriotism* to describe loyalty to your nation over loyalty to your state. It is based on the Latin word for a "country," and it soon captured the hearts and minds of the new national citizens. Underpinned with flags and emotional songs, patriots endured any hardship, including death, for their "country."

I wondered what would be a word for loyalty to the planet. Not finding one in the dictionary, I took the Greek root of the word "earth", *eraze*, and coined the word *eracism* (AIR'-uh-cism). The idea of planetary loyalty is beginning to flower all over the globe, and millions of people are enduring all kinds of hardships, including death, for the welfare of our true nation, the Earth.

The central question of this book is: What is the role that we, as individuals, are playing? Are we part of the problem or part of the solution? We have only a short period of time to decide whether we will move to a future of unparalleled peace and prosperity or to extinction.

—Michael Kessler
Louisville, KY

CHAPTER ONE

▼

KESSLER'S KWOTES

If the human race is to survive, it will require a different way of thinking.

—Albert Einstein

The artist frequently conceives of a unique pattern in his imagination before the scientist finds it objectively in nature

—R. Buckminster Fuller

The years have passed so quickly
One thing I've understood
I am only learning
To tell the trees from wood.

—John Lennon

History is bunk.

—*Henry Ford*

This time, like all times, is a very good one, if we but know what to do with it.

—*Ralph Waldo Emerson*

We are told about the world before we see it. We imagine most things before we experience them.

—*Walter Lippman*

Study the masters…every day you miss is a day you are behind.

—*Jerry Hopkins*

CHAPTER ONE

▼

THE OVERTURE

Have you ever heard of Giordano Bruno? He lived at the same time as Galileo. In 1600, Giordano was arrested, tried, and convicted by the legal authorities, taken to the center of town, and burned to death for ideas he was spreading.

And do you know what Giordano was barbecued for? He was telling people that the world was round! He said the sun is only another star and that the earth was orbiting around it! He even said that the earth is only one of a number of planets in the universe that have intelligent life!

"So what?" you say. Those people believed ideas of reality that were untrue and they burned Giordano out of superstitious fear. However, have you ever thought that you and I believe ideas that are just as untrue?

Every reader in the Christian world was raised with the belief in Santa Claus. We honestly thought that there was this happy little fat guy living at the North Pole making toys to take to children all over the world on Christmas Eve. We also thought he had a staff of elves and a team of reindeer that flew through the sky pulling Santa and his sleigh. I am sure every other culture on this planet has similar traditions.

But after we got a little older, we learned what we thought to be reality was only make-believe ideas taught to us by our society. And they were taught to us by the people we trusted the most: our mothers and fathers, our grandparents, our teachers, and our ministers. We learned sadly there is no Santa Claus, Easter Bunny, or Tooth Fairy.

Here is a story about outdated tradition. A couple were cooking a ham. It seems that while one spouse watched, the other, with great effort, removed the bone from the ham. The observer saw how much trouble that was and asked, "Why go through all of that trouble to take out the bone?"

"That is the correct way to cook ham," came the reply. "My parents taught me how to cook. This is the right way to cook a ham."

Well, now the observer's curiosity was keenly aroused. They went to their in-laws and asked them why the bone should be removed from the ham before cooking it. The in-laws thought it was a sillier question than did their child, and simply replied, being as polite as they could, that *their* parents had taught them that was the correct way.

Our observer was more curious than ever. Luckily one of the grandparents was still alive. They hurried over to ask them about removing the bone before cooking the ham.

"I just watched your grandkid remove the bone from a ham and asked them why they do that. They answered it was the correct way to cook a ham because that is the way their parents had taught them. When I went and asked the parents, they told me it was the correct way because that is the way you taught them. It looks like a lot of trouble to me."

"Oh, I agree!" the grandparent speedily replied. "The only reason I ever removed the bone in the first place was that I had a pan that was too short!"

Traditions get started sometimes for very practical reasons but often outlive their usefulness. In time they become a drawback in the solving of the problems for which they were created. Our present traditions, our *way of thinking*, were all begun in a time when they were thought to be the best way of doing things. But now they have become outdated by the information explosion begun in the 20th century. More than that, now they are themselves problems.

The outdated belief that the world is flat was replaced by the works of Giordano, Galileo, Copernicus, Columbus, and many others. Their new information ended traditions that had been accepted as reality for over hundreds of years. The reality of a round world orbiting the sun has been our reality for nearly 500 years. Now, with the works of Einstein, Fuller, and many others, the twentieth-century explosion of knowledge means we too have been given an opportunity to create a whole new reality for everyone on Earth.

Alvin Toffler, in *The Third Wave*, outlines the process this way: In the past, there were two other periods of time when one reality gave way to another very different one. Our first reality was the Stone Age, when we hunted any living thing we could catch and ate it. We also picked what nuts and berries we could find and ate them. This first reality lasted from our appearance on the planet until about 10,000 years ago.

About then, Toffler says, there was a wave of change, a transformation, that took us from hunting to farming. We tamed animals for food and to help with the work. Gradually all over the earth people settled down into villages to grow crops and tend herds. This was the first wave of change and the beginning of the second reality for us on this planet, the Age of Agriculture.

The second wave of change, from farming to industry, took place about 500 years ago during the time the powers that be were roasting Giordano. People began to learn something of the machinelike nature of the universe and made machines of their own to help with the work. Because these machines are run on fossil fuels, I call this reality the Oil Age.

What we are now going through, according to Toffler, is the third wave of change. We are seeing the dawn of our fourth reality, which I call the Solar Age, in which we are seeing the birth of a whole new human epoch.

There is a deadly side to our wave of change that was not present in the previous transitions. And it lies in our outdated traditions, in our *way of thinking*. The Stone Age *way of thinking* provides an unending period of living that almost never changes and has little impact on the environment.

Some people are now living little differently than their ancestors did 40,000 years ago.

Much the same thing holds true for people who lived in the pre-Oil Age farming reality. Using animal power and simple tools, they raised what crops they could to survive. Their impact on the environment was also very slight. They too maintained a lifestyle that changed little over several generations.

But there is a *way of thinking* in the Oil Age that is having a powerful impact on our environment. And unless this *way of thinking* is corrected very soon, the problems we are creating will mean the death of this planet. Our outdated Oil Age traditions, once useful, are eliminating our planet's ability to support us as a life-form.

There is a way we think, you and I, that is making our air unbreathable. There is a way we think, you and I, that is making our water undrinkable. There is a way we think, you and I, that is making our fertile topsoil disappear. There is a way we think, you and I, that enslaves us to joyless jobs and reduces our lives primarily to working for a living and paying bills. There is a way we think, you and I, that every year is starving to death millions of people, mostly small children and infants. There is a way we think, you and I, that is creating constant warfare all over the world. We have massacred millions of us in this century alone, and now we threaten to kill the planet itself. Einstein said that if the human race is to survive, it will require a *new way of thinking*; the Oil Age level of thinking that created our problems is not able to solve them.

When people thought the world was flat, they worked very hard to get the things they wanted in life. But that *way of thinking* had its limits. If they wanted more, then they had to leave the flat world reality and enter into the Oil Age. The same is true for us. If we want to solve our Oil Age problems and have the things we want in life, then we have to leave our outdated Oil Age *way of thinking* behind and enter the Solar Age.

In order to test these outdated traditions, I employ *semantics*, the meaning of words. The definitions we use tell us what something is. And what we think something *is* impacts our *experience* of that thing. And the experiences we have make up the *reality* of our lives.

In the Stone Age, for example, food was defined as meat, nuts, and berries. All of the remaining plants were considered weeds and not food. When Uglug, the caveman, got hungry, what showed up on the menu was some animal and a few nuts and berries. The things they called weeds did not even enter into solving the problem of hunger.

Over time and most likely through the efforts of Mrs. Uglug and the kids, people learned how plants grew and that many of them could be eaten. What they as hunters had called weeds was now a new food source: rice, corn, barley, wheat, and a host of other foods. The plants had not changed, the *way of thinking* had been *transformed*.

People can live very successful lives as hunters but never know the joys of bread, corn on the cob, rice pudding, or any of the "weeds" they are trampling on while chasing animal prey. Their experiences of reality, their very reality itself, are limited by the words they use.

Some people today still regard animals as food. Although animal nutrition has been a tradition for nearly as long as we have been on this planet, the factory production of animals in the Oil Age is an altogether different question. Whereas we once killed only a small part of the wildlife around us as hunters or butchered a small number of tamed animals as farmers, we now, machinelike, process millions of animals every day.

The factory system of animal nutrition consumes most of the vegetable nutrition we grow and most of our fresh water. It is a major source of water pollution on the planet and is the root cause of many of the diseases that kill us. It is the underlying cause of the world's hunger and poverty, which are primary sources of war. If you want to do one single thing to improve the quality of your personal life and that of the world, stop eating animals and their products.

So each reality is framed by traditions based on the meanings of words. They create a context, a space, in which the reality operates and in which we live out our lives. What we think of as true and false, real and unreal, possible and impossible, are all contained in our traditions. There are many kinds of cultures, languages, religions, and customs, but they all exist inside these commonly held traditions. Change tradition and we transform reality.

Gerald Mische, of Global Education Associates, tells a story about the limiting effects of outdated traditions:

Once there was a traveler who landed on an undiscovered planet. The planet was very lovely with many different kinds of plants and animals. The people living on the planet also were very lovely and friendly. Everything was fine, except all of the people were wearing jackets that were several sizes too small for them.

The jackets appeared to have been good looking when they were new and actually fit the wearers. But as time passed, the people continued to grow, while the jackets, of course, stayed the same. By the time the wearers reached adulthood, the jackets had become so tight that the people could hardly move. Their garments had become straightjackets.

The people's arms stuck out of the sides like scarecrows, and the buttons were so tight they could barely breathe. The colors had faded so much that sometimes it was hard to tell from a distance that the citizens of this little planet even had jackets on. There was an air of invisibility about these jackets. The most accurate way of telling what kind of jacket a person was wearing was how the person behaved.

Our traveler went up to one of the inhabitants and asked: "Excuse me, but I could not help but notice that all of the people here are wearing jackets that are far too tight for them. Could you tell me why?"

"Well," came the puzzled reply, "these beautiful jackets, which we all love and will fight and die for, were given to us at birth by our parents. Each of us gets our own color and pattern. The jackets let us know who we are and where we belong."

"But," continued the traveler, "they seem so confining. They are so small that you can hardly move or breathe freely. Why don't you take them off?"

"What?! Take them off?" the citizen said in astonishment. "These jackets have been handed down over thousands of years to us. People have struggled and died so that we might have these jackets. We must wear them with pride until we die and make sure our children wear their jackets. It has been this way forever. You must be crazy to think we can ever take our jackets off!"

The traveler really did not understand and felt sorry for the people on this isolated little world. Life for all of them would be so much more fun without the confining jackets. The people evidently did not realize what they were missing by being tied up in the outdated tradition about their jackets. Giving a sigh, the traveler turned to leave. Walking slowly away, the traveler thought they could hear the sound of something tearing....

The jackets of our outdated traditions have also become too tight. This *way of thinking* that served us over the past 500 years is now confining us and has become a threat to our survival. It has become our straightjacket.

We will examine reality as being formed by what we have been taught to be true in four main areas. The first is nature (physics), or the way we think about the world and the universe around us. We will compare the ideas about nature from the Oil Age with the new ideas of Einstein and Fuller. This new way of looking at nature quickly reveals how hampering our straightjacket thinking from the past really is.

Next we will take a look at biology, or how we define ourselves, and at economics, or what we think of as valuable. As we shall see, the truth has little to do with what we have been taught.

The main focus is on politics, about how we organize society. We have been told for centuries that society must operate within the confines of "countries." This outdated, straightjacket tradition is the main problem facing us today. And around the world you can hear the sound of it tearing.

CHAPTER TWO

▼

KESSLER'S KWOTES

I rarely think in words at all.

—Albert Einstein

Up to the Twentieth Century reality was everything humans could touch, smell, see, and hear. Now humans have learned that what they can touch, smell, see and hear is less than 1/1,000,000th of reality.

—R. Buckminster Fuller

If there is intelligent life in the universe, they are using Earth as an insane asylum.

—Bertrand Russell

All the world's a stage and we are merely players.

—*William Shakespeare*

By Man, I mean both man and woman; these are the twin exponents of a divine thought.

—*Margaret Fuller*

CHAPTER TWO

▼

HUMAN REALITY, HUMAN IDENTITY, HUMAN WEALTH

HUMAN REALITY

Using Toffler's idea of one reality giving way to another, we can see that, as information grows, so does our ability to acquire a more accurate picture of nature. But it has only been in this century that we have been able to get a picture that is in focus. Now we have entered a door to what is real and are leaving what we have been taught.

Up until Einstein, ideas of nature's reality were based upon some kind of observation. Our first reality, the Stone Age, was based on observations using our five senses. People looked around and created colorful stories about how nature works. This type of reality, called animism, says everything has a spirit of its own. Even rocks have a spiritual essence of their own. When we get to examining Einstein, we will see that although our predecessors' descriptions may not have been accurate, their insight was.

After the first wave of change took us from hunting to farming, people learned to understand their environment a little. They found that many mysteries could be explained and even controlled. They began to view nature as something being run by laws rather than by whim.

However, the observations they made were also only with their five senses. Although they were scientific in their thinking, their observations were no more accurate than Stone Age descriptions. They saw the world as flat and standing still. The rest of the universe was in orbit around the Earth. After all, that is the way it looks when you observe the universe with your own eyes.

In appearance, the Earth does look like its the center of everything. The sun obviously rises in the east, travels through the sky, and sets in the west. The moon, the planets, the very heavens themselves rotate around us! This picture of reality ruled the thinking of people for thousands of years and, as we shall see, still lives in the meanings of the words we use today.

This tradition of reality was supported by all the leaders of society. Political and religious leaders found it very useful in keeping their positions of authority. But eventually the unending growth of human learning finally caught up with them. Inventions designed to increase the power of our five senses unraveled the flat world reality. The telescope was many times more accurate than any human eye and what it saw quickly made reliance on the eye outdated.

The official line was that everything rotated around a stationary, flat Earth. Moreover, the world was said to be made of imperfect matter and the rest of the universe was made of perfect matter. With the arrival of the telescope and with observations made by people like the Polish astronomer Copernicus and the Italian genius Galileo, a whole new reality came into view.

The telescope revealed the earth to be only one of a number of planets orbiting our sun, and it to be just one of countless stars. Not only that, some of the other planets like Jupiter and Saturn had moons of their own orbiting them.

The telescope also showed that the Earth's moon is pockmarked with craters and has mountains like here on Earth. The flat areas of the moon, thought Galileo, were seas. The moon did not seem all that different from the earth and certainly was not perfect like everyone had been taught.

What had been reality for centuries was now only outdated tradition. The new observations tore off the farming reality straightjackets and replaced them with Oil Age ones.

In 1905, Albert Einstein transformed reality again with an accurateness that went far beyond what could be described by any kind of observation. Einstein's theory of relativity, based on mathematics, showed that the universe was not something merely to be observed. He discovered that the universe is an activity *to be understood*. It is *doing* something.

The three older realities that were based on observation tried to describe nature by its appearance. The importance of Einstein is that we have a breakthrough into how the universe *works* instead of just how it looks. We now have an understanding of the basic laws, which Fuller called "general operating principles," that run the *whole* universe. We can now create our future instead of relying on old trial and error methods or fate.

Someone once said that to explain Einstein in any terms but mathematics is like interpreting Beethoven on a tuba. However, we can get a basic understanding of his work to draw out the differences between what is actually going on here instead of what we were taught.

Einstein's equation, E=mc2, describes nature as energy in the form of light. This energy exists in one of two basic forms. The "E" stands for *active* light, such as is coming out of the stars. The "mc2" part stands for *stored* light, which is all of the matter of the universe. Einstein's little equation showed that light energy is 100 percent efficiently flowing from one form to the other.

Light makes up all of the universe and has developed into three basic forms: electrons, protons, and neutrons. As these collide in space, they stick together to form 92 basic elements. For example, if one electron sticks with one proton, you get one atom of the element of hydrogen. Add more electrons, protons, and neutrons and you get more elements.

Gravity draws these elements into large clouds. As the cloud becomes larger and denser, the center of it begins to burn and release its stored light. The elements become so compact from the force of gravity that the atoms collide, exploding to make new elements. Along with the active light, loose electrons, protons, and neutrons are shot into space and begin sticking with other loose electrons, protons, and neutrons to start the process all over again.

The center of the cloud, of course, becomes a star, like our sun. The rest of the cloud not in the star forms planets, moons, asteroids, comets, and loose rocks. All of this goes into making a solar system. Our star and all of the other stars were made in this manner. Our star and all of the stuff orbiting it are only one local example of what is going on everywhere in the universe.

Fuller goes on to describe this process in greater detail. Some stars' light hit planets that have the correct blend of the 92 basic elements to make DNA. This unique combination of energy and elements is called life. As the local star continues to pour light onto the planet, more and more complex forms of life develop. Eventually one life-form emerges from this life system, this ecosystem, with the ability of *creativity*. This life form is called *human* and is the way the universe thinks. The stars are the *uncontrolled, undirected* flow of energy in nature, and we humans are the *directed, creative* flow of energy.

When we thought the world was flat, all of our thinking was tied to the land. The oceans were just a vast area full of danger. We never took the seas seriously in our problem- solving. This *landbound* thinking was the foundation of what was called reality. And this *way of thinking* has become a holdover from the past and a straightjacket in our reality.

Have you ever seen a beautiful sunrise or sunset? Have you ever looked up at the moon on a clear night? Or have you ever been away from the city on a clear night and looked into outer space at the stars? In the Einstein/Fuller universe, all of that is impossible to do! Here is why:

Obviously the sun is not moving in such a way that it rises in the east and sets in the west. It just looks that way because we see the earth as standing still and see the sun as moving. However, we do not yet have the experience of cruising 60,000 miles an hour around the sun or spinning 1,000 miles an hour on our axis. We still see reality the same way as the people who burned Giordano. We see the earth as flat, standing still with the sun moving through the sky. Our words act like a filter that warps what is really happening.

The same holds true about looking up at the moon. As seen by the farming, flat-world reality, the earth was inside something called sky. Stuck on the sky was the sun, the moon, and everything else. In other words, there was one surface you were standing on and another one that you looked up at. It was much like a floor and a ceiling.

But in real space, as Fuller points out, there is no surface *up* there. He says we are on a ball in space and there are only three ways we can travel. We can travel away from it, towards it, or around it. There is no up and down in the real universe. When you look at the moon, you are really looking away from the Earth out into space.

And why can you not look into outer space at the stars? There is no outer space! There is only space and we are in it. We are in the same space as the stars, and the moon, all of the planets, and everything else.

The total effect of these outdated terms is a limiting effect on our thinking. Just like the flat-world thinkers had landbound thinking, we have *planetbound thinking*. We are standing on the shores of the real universe, but just as the flat-worlders saw the oceans as threatening, we see space as dangerous and alien. However, if we free our thinking, we realize for the first time since the Stone Age, we have information that unites us to the whole universe with all of its wealth and adventure.

Now that we know the universe is creating limitless planets with ecosystems that produce humans, we need to take a short look at another one of these rules that run nature: a little rule that is called the attrition rate in nature.

Simply put, not all things that are born survive. For example, of all the robins that hatch, 90 percent just fall out of the nest. Of the remaining 10 percent, many get eaten by predators, shot by pellet rifles, or run over by cars and lawnmowers. Of the original 100 percent to hatch, perhaps 5 percent survive to carry on the species. And look how many robins there are!

In the Einstein/Fuller universe these same proportions apply to planets. Of the 100 percent of planets that develop humans, only a small number are successful. Some planets originate around a star that explodes and the experiment goes bust there. Some have their humans pop out on a planet with an unstable core and it blows up along with all of its humans. And still others come into the gravity field of another piece of space real estate like our moon. Instead of getting into an orbital dance, these worlds collide, killing all life on them.

Last, some humans develop where the planet and star are both stable. There are one or more moons peacefully orbiting the planet. But the humans there are so tightly trapped in the straightjackets of their outdated traditions, they blow themselves up or destroy their ecosystem to the point where it cannot support them any longer.

But the humans that emerge on about 5 percent of the planets in the universe are successful. They take the information of their Einsteins and Fullers and create a global reality of peace and prosperity. These humans live in the real universe, leave their outdated traditions behind, and enjoy a life of peace and abundance.

We humans on planet Earth are at the crossroads as to which way we will go. Either our outdated traditions are obsolete or we are.

HUMAN IDENTITY

Recognizing that our thinking is planetbound and based on appearance, it is little wonder that our thinking about everything else has been wrong. In this section we examine ideas of who we say we are. We look at three major areas: who we are physically (biology), who we are mentally (psychology), and who we are ontologically (spirit).

Physical Identity

Charles Darwin is widely considered the founder of modern biology with his work on evolution. He concluded humans are just another species among all of the other species on earth, described by their physical appearance and history. All of biology since Darwin has concentrated on the history and development of humans as an animal species.

But humans, in the Solar Age reality of Einstein and Fuller, are described as *energy beings of creativity*. The rules that run the universe create humans by the caseload. In an endless variety of bodies and species, they and we are human because we have the power of creativity. It just so happens we humans on planet Earth took the form of primates.

If the dinosaurs had not gone extinct, they most likely would have become the humans on this planet. In place of our apelike bodies, we would have sleek reptile ones. Our diets would be different too. Instead of eating dead animals, we would be devouring live mice and rats. But we would still be human because of our power of creativity.

In the American television series *Star Trek*, there was an episode involving people on a mining planet being attacked and killed by a horrible monster. This demon oozed an acid that allowed it to travel through rock like we walk through air. After it had been wounded, Spock, himself from a planet other than Earth, made a mental contact with the monster.

It turns out the miners had dug into the nursery where the silicon eggs were to hatch and continue the survival of the "monsters" on this planet. They called themselves hortas. Although the horta was a species made out of silicon and not carbon like we are, it possessed the power of creativity and thus was human.

Seeing ourselves as a species is the foundation of other incorrect thinking, such as speaking of ourselves in terms of race,gender,and age. We really do not talk about ourselves at the human level as a rule. That identification remains like an invisible background against which we paint our everyday lives.

For example, to European colonists, the Native Americans all pretty much looked alike physically and used secondary traits to describe themselves. They primarily identified themselves by their tribal membership. That idea worked fine until people who were not native came onto the scene. The Europeans did not care about which tribe the Native Americans said they belonged. The newcomers dealt with all tribes as one group: Indians. The Native Americans' failure to overcome their tribal thinking was a major factor in their downfall.

We are doing the very same thing. We chiefly talk about ourselves according to secondary, subhuman traits. Instead of realizing we are humans (*energy beings of creativity*), we strut around bragging that we are white, black, brown, yellow, or whatever. We really do think we are simply our bodies and say we are male, female, gay, or some mixture of sexual identification. And then we gripe about our age, saying we are old, young, or somewhere in between. We are still rooted in appearance thinking, held over from our past two realities.

Imagine you are sitting with me somewhere and I pull out a small death-dealing device. If I touch you with it, you will die. I try and miss. You have now just had a near- fatal experience. At this point, in walks the person you love most in life. This favorite person has a burning desire to talk to me. You know that if this happens, I will kill them with my death-dealing device. What do you do?

You share your experience by yelling: "Look out, this turkey's got a death-dealing device!" At that instant your loved one has a new bit of information to add to their original idea of coming to talk to me. Between the new information and the original idea lies the space where your loved one will decide what they will do. Our power to share experience and create solutions is our human identity.

Plants and animals do not have this power and each must pass or fail the death experiences on their own. Humans can anticipate and create whatever they need. As Fuller said, humans are the way the universe makes order out of chaos. Darwin left this out completely. He said we are subject to the same rule book as the other species.

Mental Identity

After our outdated belief that we are an animal species, our psychological personality emerges as the next major identity. Freud, believing we are a species, divided our mental self into three basic units. The first, the id, holds all of our survival needs, such as for food. Next we develop the ego (our personality) to satisfy the needs of the id. Freud concludes by saying the solutions the ego comes up with are measured against the super-ego, which contains the rules of right and wrong of the society into which we are born.

Martin Heidegger expanded the picture of the personality in his explanation about the mind. He said that when we are born, we are involuntarily thrown into a period of history and waiting for us is a whole set of traditions to tell us what everything is.

It is a complete package of traditions with our name on it. Regardless of whether we are born into a hunting, farming, or Oil Age society, we all immediately undergo intense brainwashing to make us acceptable members of that society.

At the same time we have personal experiences that leave permanent memories. Heidegger listed as the most influential experiences the ones we think are life threatening, that involve sudden losses, or are a combination of these two.

According to Heidegger, each of these experiences is stored in our personality's memory. Every sight, sound, smell, taste, air pressure, humidity, and emotion is stored for immediate recall should we face similar experiences again.

The mind uses these memories for one reason: *our survival.* The mind tells us how to act, talk, walk, and think so that we can make it in our society. The result of this brainwashing and our own experiences is the creation of a personality. From mass murderers to saints, we all put together an image that we think will get us through life safely.

Try this little experiment. Recall your first memory. Go back to the earliest thing you can remember. Was the memory before your fifth birthday? Was it around your third birthday? Most people who do this answer yes. We are beginning to understand that everyone born on Earth undergoes the same process in developing their personality.

For it is during this time that some experience occurs that makes our personality go vocal. We are told the little voice in our heads is us thinking. Actually it is our manufactured personality, our survival tool, talking *to* us. The voice recites nonstop to us the traditions of our society mixed in with solutions developed from the memories of our personal experiences.

But observe a child under the age of three. The younger the better because children are closer to what we really are when we are born: human. Children under three do not behave as if they are their bodies at all. They do not do anything according to the idea they are a gender, race, or age. They behave out of their nature as playful, *energy beings of creativity*. Their bodies are not who they are but only something they carry around.

We live out our whole lives like caterpillars in a cocoon, but never flying free of it. Imprisoned in our outdated traditions, we bend our lives to fit ideas no longer true. The time has come to divorce ourselves from our outdated *way of thinking* and begin to discover everything anew. The definitions we were given at birth are obsolete. We now have the opportunity to begin all over.

Fuller said we are born as the product of over four billion years of development to be total successes here. However, immediately after birth we enter into a "de-geniusizing process" that results in our imprisonment. It seems that instead of *developing* into adults, we *degenerate* into them. Instead of life continuing to be unending discovery, it becomes a well-defined rule book which we obey without question.

Einstein was asked, shortly before his death, what he thought about dying. He replied that for those who knew, this life is just an illusion, although a persistent one. These persistent illusions are our outdated, subhuman *way of thinking*. These fairy tales that we are our bodies, that we live in "countries" and belong to some sort of race, gender, or age, are the straightjackets given to us at birth. We live our whole lives in make-believe.

We humans are not born to be trapped in a fear-based life of survival. That is life at the animal level. Do not animals have personalities? Do not animals have intelligence? Do not animals have race, gender, and age? These are not the way to identify *humans*.

To define humans accurately, we cannot look to our bodies. They are only the chance product of this planet's ecosystem. We cannot look to our personalities. They are only mental survival tools based on our society's traditions and our personal experiences after birth. If we want a true definition of who we humans are, we must look at what makes us different.

Spiritual Reality

Remember how the Stone Age people said everything has its own spirit? Einstein and Fuller have elevated science to the level of spirit. There is an energy that is peculiar to everything. Simple matter has energy that is only basic atoms. But other things have a higher energy, a peculiar thing called life. Plants and animals have an energy that makes them what they are.

And there is an energy, a spirit, that makes us *human*. In fact, this energy lifts us out of the ecosystem altogether. Our conscious energy, our *creativity*, our soul, our spirit, is divine and eternal. When we see through the masks of race, gender, age, and personality, we connect with the energy that is all of us.

Imagine you are swimming in any ocean of the world and a very large, triangular fin emerges out of the water and is headed straight for you.

Most likely you will discover spirit right then and there by deciding you are about to be eaten by a shark. Race probably will not have much interest for you, since you will care little if it is a white, blue, mako, hammerhead, or tiger shark. And you also will not be too much occupied with the gender of the shark, overlooking whether if it is a male, female, or gay shark. The age of the shark will not be of much importance. Who cares if it is a young, teen-aged, middle-aged, or senior citizen shark? The personality of the shark will not be of much concern. And you can rest assured the shark also will not be interested in that stuff either. It will be dealing with you at the level of spirit too: You are lunch!

So spirit defines things at the level of what something *is* and not with how it *appears*. If you hear the word "tree," any one of a thousand kind of trees can come to mind, but they are all trees because they share the same characteristics of trees. Say the word "cat" and creatures from cute little housepets to saber-toothed tigers come to mind. They are different species, sexes, and personalities, but they are all the same kinds of beings: cats.

It is the same for humans. Remember Einstein and Fuller's universe is creating humans: *energy beings of creativity.* There are minerals, plants, and animals, and now there is a separate group, we humans. We are not another kind of animal. We are a whole new form of life altogether.

One human characteristic of human creativity is the ability to envision a future and then bring it into existence. From the first simple tools to landing on the moon, the history of humans on this planet has been one of creation: tools, language, mathematics, science, and art.

Fuller said humans cannot learn less. Moment by moment information is fed into our creativity for solutions that exceed the limitations of the instinct levels of plants and animals. With the information explosion of the twentieth century now at our disposal, we have available solutions once thought impossible. We *now* have the ability to grow enough food to feed everyone. We *now* can provide health care to everyone. We *now* can liberate everyone from drudgery. The only thing standing in our way is our outdated *way of thinking*. Combine our spiritual *intellgence with creativity* with the new opportunities and possibilities of Einstein and Fuller, and life on Earth becomes a whole different story.

HUMAN WEALTH

How does our planet-bound thinking affect our ideas about wealth (economics)? Take something regarded as valuable, such as gold, and ask yourself why it was chosen to be valuable in the first place. At the outset its characteristics may come to mind. It is pretty, which goes along with our history of judging things by appearance. It is also easily shaped so that we can make pretty things out of it. Gold does not rust or decay, which is good when one is thinking of making things to last such as money or jewelry. However, none of this is the real reason why gold is considered valuable.

Gold, like all precious metals and jewels, is valuable because it is *rare*. But it is rare only if you think of Earth as the one place where gold is found. And with the planetbound thinking of everyone before our century, that is exactly what is thought to be true.

In the Solar Age reality of Einstein and Fuller, remember, the whole universe is made up of only 92 elements. The entire universe is just these elements in a constant state of recycling. That means that gold is only one of these 92 elements and it is scattered throughout the universe.

There is undoubtedly gold on the moon, Mars and all of the planets. An asteroid passed within 20 million miles of Earth in the early 1990s. That is about the same distance to Venus, on which we have landed spacecraft. This asteroid had over a trillion dollars' worth of gold in it. There was also several trillion dollars of platinum in it. And when some meteorites have been broken, they were discovered to contain diamond dust. The real universe contains an abundance of all the stuff that we, with our planetbound thinking, think is rare and valuable.

The outdated tradition that runs our thinking about wealth therefore is *scarcity*. Seeing our planet as our only resource base presents us with a reality where we must struggle and compete, like Darwin's plants and animals, over a limited supply of the things we need to survive.

This tradition has created a dog-eat-dog reality for the whole world. We starve to death millions of people a year, mostly small children, and do not blink an eye. We slave our lives away at joyless jobs, casually calling it the real world, and there is nothing we can do about it.

Scarcity thinking has been the curse of our existence since we emerged from this planet's ecosystem. Hunting cultures had so little they carried everything they owned around with them. Their economic system, called bartering, was based on trading your stuff for some of someone else's stuff.

When farming replaced hunting, people settled down near their crops and collected more stuff than they could carry with them. They solved the problem by taking something rare, like gold, to represent the value of their real stuff. This was easily carried and could be traded for the stuff they needed or wanted. This was the birth of money. Now our whole lives are dominated by the imaginary necessity to earn money to live.

Scarcity thinking has its ultimate expression in the theories of capitalism and communism. Adam Smith, with his planetbound scarcity thinking, founded capitalism in the eighteenth century. Karl Marx, with his planetbound scarcity thinking, founded communism a few years later in the middle of the nineteenth century.

Smith said it is obvious there is not enough to go around and concluded that we must struggle against one another for our share. If you happen to fall into the class of have-nots, tough luck. Marx thought that was unfair and said the have-nots, for him the industrial workers, should have a violent revolution to grab the wealth from the haves, the industrial owners, and share it equally with everyone. Then everyone will at least have what they need to survive. But the first false step in these ideas is that there is scarcity in the first place.

In the Solar Age reality of Einstein and Fuller, there is not a lack of anything. Scarcity, like believing the world is flat, exists only in our minds, not in reality. For the first time in human history on this planet, we are able to use ideas of wealth based upon *abundance*.

With the unlimited resources of the real universe and the employment of Solar Age technology, we can create a world where our lives are not about struggles for survival but about individual struggles to be the best us that we can be. We now can create a prosperous planet that runs in harmony with nature rather than at the present expense of it.

Einstein and Fuller have shown that the universe *is* technology. The energy that is everything is in a 100 percent efficient flow with nothing being lost. We operate on the belief that we must find scarce raw materials, make them into usable products, and then throw what is left into our water, air, or landfills. After using the products, we also throw them away and then go looking for more raw materials.

The error in that kind of thinking is filling all of our waste dumps to excess, turning our fresh water into acid, heating up our atmosphere, and spoiling our land and air. It is killing the oceans upon which all life on Earth depends. It is wiping out the tropical rainforests with all of its oxygen production and life forms. It is more and more rapidly bringing life on this planet closer and closer to extinction. Either our Oil Age *way of thinking* about economics is obsolete or we are.

Fuller created Design Science based on the abundance of the universe. It recognizes the reality of unlimited resources from the sheer immensity of the universe and its 92 recycling elements. The universe uses and reuses all of the existing elements and their parts to provide an unending supply. If we operate our economic thinking to equal that of the real universe, we can provide wealth for us all at the same level that we have air.

For example, it takes about ten cents of energy to make an aluminum can. It takes about one penny to recycle that can into another can. Nine cents of energy are saved and can be directed into other uses, like paying our bills. And we still have all the cans we need.

The truth is that there is no way for us not to recycle. The only question is how we recycle. We can recycle by dumping everything into the environment, or we can use our resources so that they will flow like the rivers and not become pollution to kill the planet.

Design Science sees the universe as *the* master system of which we are a very small part. The rules that run this system also run all of the parts, including our planet. To ignore these rules is like trying to jump off a skyscraper and ignore gravity. The rules of the universe operate whether we like them or not. They work whether we know about them or not. Understanding them and using them mean an opportunity to put more money in our pockets and more paid holidays on our calendar.

Fuller spent 55 years of his life designing a technology based upon Einstein's universe. The core of his work is wrapped up in the word *synergetics*. Simply put, synergetics is the fact that things working together can produce more than things working separately.

We live in the outdated tradition that competition is the driving force of progress. But in a universe of recycling wealth, cooperation is much more productive. Imagine two people in a rowboat race and each competing with the rowing of the boat. The boat may move forward but will move only poorly. But if the two rowers work in cooperation, the boat will glide swiftly and smoothly through the water. The same holds true for humans rowing a planet.

From synergetics Fuller created low cost housing that can provide shelter for everyone on Earth. In the 1930s he brought forth advances such as aerodynamic design and front wheel drive for automobiles. His Dymaxion™ car held over twelve people and did over one hundred miles an hour on a seventy-five horsepower engine. His developments in architecture produced the geodesic dome which covers the largest area with the least materials.

In Chapter Five, we discuss Fuller's Global Grid Project. This electrical transmission system is designed to harness the awesome power that is the universe, distribute it throughout the world, and lay the foundation for a prosperous civilization unheard of in the history of the planet.

CHAPTER THREE

▼

KESSLER'S KWOTES

The atom bomb changed everything except the way we think.
—Albert Einstein

Only complete de-sovereignization can permit the realization of an all humanity high standard support.
—R. Buckminster Fuller

My country is the world.
—Thomas Paine

When you find yourself on the side of the majority, it's time to switch sides.
—Mark Twain

Let us put our minds together and see what life we will make for our children.

—*Tatanka Yotanka(Sitting Bull)*

Peace is more than the absence of tension. It is the presence of justice.

—*Martin Luther King, Jr.*

CHAPTER THREE

▼

HUMAN SOCIETY

In 1968, the Apollo VIII spacecraft headed toward the moon. It was the first vessel with humans from this planet aboard that had ever left Earth orbit. One of the crew looked back and saw something no Earth human had ever seen. And they took a picture of it.

What they photographed was our planet as it *is* in space. Before this photograph we had to use our imaginations to picture the world. Since no one had ever actually seen Earth in space, we made our maps and globes equal our outdated traditions. All of the landmass was cut up into "countries," which strengthened everyone's belief in their existence. With pretty colors showing each "country," with the "seven seas," lines of latitude and longitude, and an equator, these globes and maps supported the Oil Age idea that we only live on a piece of the planet. In fact, most people do not even talk about living on a planet at all but only about living in a "country."

In the picture from Apollo VIII there are no little dotted lines on the surface of the real planet dividing it into all kinds of make-believe pieces. What we see is our small, blue-green jewel of a planet slowly spinning around one medium-sized star. And all of this is against the immense background of the Milky Way galaxy and its billions of stars.

Of all of the outdated traditions we use to run our lives, the one that we live in "countries" is the most harmful. Our lives are dominated by the planetbound idea that we live in "countries." The joke is that we do not live in "countries" at all, but they live in us, as figments of our imaginations!

Einstein said anyone really interested in world peace should read *The Anatomy of Peace*, by Emory Reves. Reves says there is never peace *between* separate units but only *among* them. In other words, when all of the artificial pieces are tied together as one, like the states in "countries" are now, then there is peace.

And Jonathan Schell, in *The Fate of the Earth*, says that when you have a system of unconnected "countries," a part of that system is war. Without any higher authority, unconnected "countries" are free to use violence to solve their differences. It is not a question *if* there will be war but only *when* and *where*.

Schell adds that the tradition of war has been that there are enemies who fight one another with one winning and the other losing. But with the arrival of nuclear and biological weapons, we now have toys that do not play our idea of war. We may be thinking *war* but the weapons are playing *extinction*.

And we are spending two million dollars a minute on such weapons to defend the outdated idea that we live in "countries." There are enough nuclear weapons to provide an explosion worth two million tons of dynamite for everyone on Earth. As Fuller observed, either war is obsolete or we are.

Thomas Jefferson said that institutions, such as "countries," must develop "hand in hand with the progress of the human mind." Our outdated tradition of "countries" dates back hundreds of years. It is unable to go hand in hand with the progress of the Solar Age.

To handle all of that information, to develop all of that new technology, to realize all of those possibilities and opportunities, we need to create a new society. We need to create a society equal to the picture from the Apollo spacecraft. We need to create one political, social, and economic society out of our planet. We need to create a global nation with a constitution and a freely elected government.

And given the problems facing us, particularly concerning the environment, we have precious little time to lose. We cannot wait for everyone to join hands in family love and forgiveness. That will come later. But we can do what Martin Luther King, Jr. said to do. He said the law may not make you love me, but it will keep you from lynching me.

The same holds true for "countries." The only thing that has ever worked is elevating the rule book to the level of *law*. A world society needs world law. The present system of national armies has never produced peace, cannot produce peace, and never will produce peace. Unconnected "countries" will only produce what they have always produced: poverty, war, wage slavery, and now, extinction.

Einstein and Fuller have given us yardsticks to understand nature and the tools to make everyone rich. They have shown that we are one people on one planet. So what is the yardstick by which we can create a human society and turn these opportunities into realities?

In the American Declaration of Independence, Thomas Jefferson laid out the blueprint for just such a society. As Einstein laid out the rules that operate nature, so has Jefferson laid out the rules to operate a global society.

Basically, the Declaration is in four parts. The first part is a simple statement of purpose to outline the reasons why the Declaration was being written. The part we want to concentrate on is the second part, the ideas of society (see Appendix IV). The third part is merely a list of gripes against the British, especially the king. The fourth part will receive some of our attention too. It is the commitment needed to see these ideas realized. And this statement is as true today as it was in 1776.

The second section, with the ideas on government, begins with one of the most famous lines in history: "We hold these truths to be self-evident...." Now when something is self-evident, it does not have to be explained or proven. Things like gravity are self-evident. Drop a rock and gravity works without any awareness on the part of the rock. It is self-evident. Jump off a bridge and gravity will work whether you have changed your mind or not. It is self-evident. It just *is*.

The Declaration then goes on to list some of the things it considers to be self-evident truths. The first is all humans are created equal. To get to the truth of this statement, let's return to the identity part of this book.

Remember, we humans cannot be described as a species. Our bodies are only chance developments on one planet in the whole universe. There are an estimated 100 million planets in our galaxy alone that could have Earthlike conditions. And in the billions of known galaxies there are many countless possibilities on other planets. Whatever the type of body that is developed, they are obviously not equal. So the Declaration is not talking about *physical* equality.

Equality will not be found in our personalities either, especially in the light of research being done on animal intelligence. With these results, we are getting information that we need to overhaul our definitions of them and ourselves. We absolutely are not the only intelligent species on this planet. The only way we humans are different is by the type of intelligence we possess.

That brings us back to spirit. If you want to have a self-evident truth of equality, it can only be found in our essence. The universe does not play favorites. We are equal products of an equal system. We are equal because of our *humanness*. And our humanness is based on our power of *creativity*, our spirit.

The Declaration continues the self-evident truth list by saying we humans are *endowed* by our Creator "with certain inalienable rights." Now when you are endowed with something, it is yours by right of birth. You do not have to ask for it, earn it, pay for it, or beg for it. It goes along with the territory of your equality. Tigers are endowed with stripes and humans are endowed with rights.

And these rights are *inalienable*. That means they cannot be taken away from you anymore than you can take away a tiger's stripes. These rights are ours by virtue of our being human, and they are not up for discussion.

The Declaration then lists a few of these rights. It says that among these rights are "life, liberty, and the pursuit of happiness." Notice that it says *among* these. The list only contains three, but there are many more that could be added. The U.S. Constitution has the Bill of Rights and other amendments, that, like the U.N.'s Universal Declaration of Human Rights, list more rights that we all possess.

If we look at the world around us, it becomes very clear that our rights are being stepped on. As far as our right to life is concerned, we are sinking one trillion dollars a year into weapons systems, which Fuller calls "killingry." We have murdered more people in wars since World War Two than in all of that conflict. This system, combined with our primitive ideas of animal nutrition, is killing millions more through starvation and malnutrition. And we are rapidly wiping out the environment's ability to support us. Our self-evident, divinely endowed, inalienable right to life is not secure.

And the situation is no better when it comes to the question of liberty. Have you ever tried to travel from one part of the planet to another? As it was for the slaves of the American South, we have to get permission slips to travel off our plantation, our "country."

Our first permission slip comes in the form of a passport. On some parts of the planet, people must use passports even to travel within their own "country"! Birth certificates, applications, several sets of photographs, and, of course, filing fees must be submitted in correct form for approval. Then comes the visa process, more applications, pictures, filing fees, and lists of what you can do, see, say, photograph, buy, or sell. Our self-evident, divinely endowed, inalienable right to liberty is not secure.

And don't even think in terms of pursuit of happiness. Are you doing what you want, when you want, and for as long as you want? Are we living our dreams and visions now or are we trapped in an Oil Age struggle like slaves to pay bills and taxes? And what are we getting for all of our labor and sacrifice? Look at the world and tell me our pursuit of happiness has not been sacrificed on the altar of the outdated traditions of politics and economics. Our self-evident, divinely endowed, inalienable right to the pursuit of happiness is not secure.

When these ideas were first written in the Declaration of Independence, they were truly revolutionary. The popular idea then was that the rights of the people were whatever the local ruler said they were. No wonder the Declaration caught the imaginations of the oppressed people of the planet. But the real dynamite of the Declaration lies in the remaining parts of the second section.

The Declaration continues its discussion about the rights of humans and says "governments are instituted [created]" to *secure our rights*. Notice the Declaration does not say governments are to tell, grant, define, or give us our rights. They are only in existence to safeguard what is already ours by birth. All society is only a system created to do just that.

The *power* to secure our rights comes from the "consent of the governed," from *you* and *me*. Simply put, we, the people of this planet, create a government to protect our self-evident, divinely endowed, inalienable rights to life, liberty, and the pursuit of happiness. And the government has only as much power as we give it. Government makes a good servant but a poor master.

In an age when people thought power to rule came from divine sources, democracy was a threat to all existing governments. But the Declaration revealed that democracy really is the *only* kind of government. If people decide to create another form of government, there is nothing that can stop them. The way we live our lives is our vote on how we want life to be. When we, the people, act in unison for what we want, there is nothing that can stop us. Kings, tyrants, nor wealth can withstand the power of we, the people.

If we are not active citizens in the creation of our own lives, then eventually some person or group of persons will run the government their way. If that is the case, the Declaration says "whenever any government becomes destructive to [the securing of our rights], it is the *right of the people to alter or abolish it.*"

Thomas Jefferson thought there should be a revolution every twenty years or so to keep the system fined-tuned to the needs of the people. He did not mean a violent overthrow of the system, but to update it to the "progress of the human mind."

The flawed system of unconnected states was peacefully altered by the acceptance of the new American Constitution in 1787. Now all of the states were connected by law into one unit. That is the kind of revolution Jefferson meant, and that is the kind of revolution we face.

Our system of unconnected "countries" is just like the situation when the the Constitution was written. Before the Constitution, people saw themselves as living in sovereign states. And like the United Nations today, they met in a Congress that had no power to tell any member state what to do. In only four years this system began to collapse into war.

To prevent bloodshed, the creators of this system remet in Philadelphia to do what the Declaration said to do. They met to alter or abolish the existing system that was not securing their rights. They realized their only hope lay in the creation of a system that could handle their problems at the *national* level. They needed a government with *lawful* powers to handle things as one nation.

With the threat of nuclear weapons, with the horror of world hunger, malnutrition, and poverty, with the suffering of discrimination and persecution, with the fouling of our environment, and with the daily slavery of earning a living, is there any doubt that the present system of unconnected "countries" is not doing its job? Is there any doubt our rights are not secure?

The time has come for each of us to assume our democratic responsibility and to do what we know must be done. We have the right- and the *duty*, says the Declaration- to throw off the chains of these outdated traditions and provide new safeguards for securing our rights. It is time to make one nation out of the world.

In the fourth part of the Declaration, Jefferson listed the type of commitment necessary to pull this off successfully. He wrote: "…and for the support of this Declaration, with a firm reliance on the protection of

Divine Providence, we mutually pledge to each other our *lives*, our *fortunes*, and our *sacred honour*."

Gandhi said his life was the message. Each of us is voting on how we want the future to be. We all have a life, a fortune, and a sacred honor to commit. What we do and do not do adds up to what we call reality. Our common reality is a product of our individual actions.

We have all been raised with outdated traditions. If we continue to support "countries" and scarcity economics, we are voting for extinction. But if we adopt the new *way of thinking* offered by the Solar Age information of Einstein and Fuller, then we will establish a whole new era for the human race. As Fuller put it, our choice is truly utopia or oblivion.

CHAPTER FOUR

▼

KESSLER'S KWOTES

When I examine myself and my methods of thought I come to the conclusion that the gift of fantasy has meant more to me than my talent for absorbing positive knowledge.

—Albert Einstein

You can use a piano top for a life preserver in a shipwreck, but that doesn't mean the best way to design life preservers is in the form of a piano top.

—R. Buckminster Fuller

Does not the history of the world show there would have been no romance in life if there had been no risks?

—Mohandas K. Gandhi

There was a time when it was proper, and there is a time for it to cease.

—Thomas Paine

Life in the twentieth century is like a parachute jump: you have to get it right the first time.

—Margaret Mead

CHAPTER FOUR

▼

CREATING A NEW REALITY

The idea of realities coming and going rarely crosses anyone's mind. And fewer yet ever think of reality *having* to be changed. In the past, new information gradually replaced the old *way of thinking*. Our first reality, the Stone Age, was replaced slowly over the years by the farming reality. It, in turn, was taken over by our reality, the Oil Age. And given enough time, the Solar Age reality of Einstein and Fuller will push the outdated Oil Age aside.

But that is not the situation with our reality shift. We do not seem to have a great deal of time for this to occur before the damage we are doing produces extinction. The question clearly for us is not one of evolution but of *creation*. Either we create a new reality or go extinct with the old one.

Before we discuss the steps of change, let's look at the characteristics of the Oil Age and the Solar Age. Using Toffler's *The Third Wave* as the measuring stick, let's see what is the cost of the old and the promise of the new.

Toffler says our outdated Oil Age reality has six traits. The first is *standardization*. Everything is designed to conform our actions, indeed our entire lives, to a common idea of what is correct. Like the machines we serve, we are expected to fit neatly into the system, to be team players, and not to rock the boat.

In the Solar Age reality of Einstein and Fuller, the emphasis is on the individual. Our occupations and our personal likes and dislikes need no longer take a backseat to some mass opinion of what is normal.

The second trait is *specialization*. There was a time, like in the Middle Ages, when it seemed possible to acquire all of the knowledge that was then known. That is because there was so little known and the common idea was there really was that not anything new to learn.

But the Oil Age sped up the growth of information, and it blew the lid off of everything with an unheard of explosion of new knowledge. People began to limit themselves to smaller and smaller pieces of the total information pie. More and more, they became specialists in one particular field of study. Just think how specialized medicine has become and you will get the picture.

When everyone was deciding on what kind of specialist they were going to be, Fuller concluded that he was going to seek the general rules that run the universe, including all of its parts. He became a *comprehensivist* to seek out the master system that runs everything else. He once said the only reason anyone ever heard of him at all was lack of competition.

It was not long before he was studying Einstein. He quickly recognized that Einstein had discovered the very rules he was seeking. The specialists were still looking at the universe through the eyes of Newton. They were still bogged down in appearance.

They saw the universe as a machine made of an infinite number of parts. They thought if they understood all of the parts, they would eventually understand the nature of the machine. But it was Einstein who explained the universe as one unfolding system. It was this breakthrough that meant we now are in a new reality.

The third trait of the Oil Age reality is that everything is expected to run according to the same schedule. This is what Toffler calls *synchronization*. It is really a holdover from our farming reality. People had to get up early and work all day long just to make enough to survive. Lives were shaped by the schedule of the seasons. Later, in the Oil Age, people got up early and worked all day to earn enough money to survive. Time became money; no time to lose, don't be late. From the first years of school to death or retirement, we are on the clock.

The Solar Age of Einstein and Fuller offers a different set of rules. There is greater flexibility now in the workplace with the way we get things done. The arrival of personal computers means that a great deal of work can be done in your own home at 2:30 in the morning if you want. But the big carrot of the Solar Age is that now we can envision the end to earning-a-living work altogether.

Fuller said that before The Solar Age the meanings of work and labor were just about the same, but now we can draw a huge distinction between them. He said work can now be used to refer to what you *want* to do with your time and energies. Labor would refer to what you *have* to do with your time and energies in order to survive. Think of the differences between job time and vacation time, and I believe you will see the difference.

Fuller showed that the twentieth century offered us the opportunity to create a world were most of our time can be spent doing what we want and not what we have to do. This labor done by technology (what I call cybernetic slavery) operates with the powers of the universe, and can create a society so wealthy that everyone born is on a birth-to-death scholarship.

And the world, indeed the universe itself, becomes a playground. Everyone is free to pursue their personal desires. Imagine the explosive growth in science, art, sports, and everything else when we are following our dreams and not dragging ourselves off to some joyless job.

The fourth trait of the Oil Age is what Toffler calls *concentration*. This refers to the ability to focus only on one thing at a time. Similar to specialization, concentration also constricts our range of attention and activity.

In the Solar Age we are able to be more diversified, free to pursue several things at once. We are all open-ended parts of one system, able to interact with all of the other parts. We are not boxed up into artificial "countries" or business departments. We do not need to think of having to learn one skill and do that for the rest of our lives.

The fifth trait is *maximization*. In the outdated Oil Age, bigger is better. If something was huge, it must be good. As with large "countries," large corporations often swallow up the individuals who work for it. They become another cog in the machine of the company. Their specialized work isolates them and few ever get the chance to see the whole picture. Being penned up in their narrow fields of activity, they quickly feel meaningless and their personal hopes, dreams, and visions are unimportant.

In the Solar Age reality of Einstein and Fuller, maximization is replaced by synergetics, which looks at things as a system. This system connects all of the parts into a meaningful whole. The environment is a good example of synergetics. With specialized thinking, we may not see how things are connected between one part of the environment and another. But that does not mean the connection does not exist.

In outdated Oil Age thinking, unconnected individuals compete with one another for some sense of progress. The result of this attitude is the ruthless climb up the corporate ladder. The outcome of this frame of mind gets more intense when "countries" compete in war. Synergetics now shows that parts connect into one system to create peaceful cooperation and they produce more with less effort.

Last, there is *centralization*. We all go to one place to work, to another for school, and then to another for church or whatever. The ultimate place is a "country." To realize the other traits of the outdated Oil Age, people had to be herded into one place.

Power was concentrated into one city so that the whole nation could be ruled. And sometimes in the hands of one person or a small group of persons. From there, central rules (standardization) were sent on every issue (specialization), with all the issues to be settled at one time (synchronization). And everything worked to make the "country" as big and as powerful as possible (maximization).

The Solar Age allows us to explore a whole new way of living. Within a global society we are free to decentralize our power. Since all of the parts are seen as being within one planetary system, power can be distributed and shared in a variety of ways among the various parts.

The way things get done can be tailored to meet the local expressions of life, liberty, and pursuit of happiness. Local problem solvers can be free to draw upon the resources of the whole system (synergetics), and the people can be free to employ all of their talents (comprehensiveness).

Now, then, how is such a reality created? Fuller outlined in his book, *Critical Path*, the four steps he saw as necessary if life on Earth is to survive.

The first is the development of a *personal go-for-broke attitude*. Many people take a look at the evening news and are so overwhelmed by the apparent size of the problems that they say there is nothing one person can do. But the one thing we all do is decide whether to do something. The only thing we really have any control over is ourselves. For example, we can greatly improve our health, clean up the environment, save acres of the rain forest, and end death from hunger by eliminating animal nutrition in our diet. We all choose the foods we eat.

And the real truth is that there are millions of individuals all over the earth acting alone and within organizations to take care of one thing or another. The monumental changes in Europe in 1989, the end of apartheid in South Africa, and events all over the globe prove that it is only the individual that changes anything.

There is a story about a village that sat on the shore of the sea. The people were peaceful farmers who tended their corps on the hillsides overlooking the village. Every day they would hike up as one group and work all day on their crops. They all knew their individual security lay in their group efforts.

One evening after the day's work had been completed, one of the villagers decided to return to the fields on the hillsides and just make sure everything was all right. The villager was happy to see the fruits of everyone's cooperative labor. There were fields of wheat, rice, and all kinds of vegetables and fruits to feed everyone.

But as the villager returned to go home, they stopped to pause and gaze at the village itself. There they saw family and friends going about their final chores of the day before relaxing for the evening. And then turning their attention to the vast ocean, the villager was horror-struck to see a monstrous wave roaring down to drown the village!

A moment of panic soon gave way to thoughts of how to warn friends and loved ones in time so that they might be saved. There was not enough time to run down there and get everyone to safety. The village was also too far away to shout any warnings. It looked like there was nothing to do but stand there and watch home, family, and friends be destroyed.

Then the villager had an impossible idea. They set fire to the wheat field! The flames were quickly fanned by the sea breezes and it was not long before a huge fire was burning out of control. As soon as the rest of the villagers discovered the disaster, everyone rushed out as quickly as they could to put out this threat to their food supply. When they got there, they found out they had also saved themselves from drowning from the mountain of water that was now wiping out their village.

There is a tidal wave of environmental destruction, a tidal wave of nuclear, chemical, and biological extinction, a tidal wave of hunger and starvation roaring down on us too. The question is, are we going to stand frozen in our tracks, or are we going to do something about it?

Ken Keyes wrote a splendid book called *The Hundredth Monkey* to make people aware of the nuclear wave threatening us and what can be done to stop it. In the book he described an experiment in which monkeys on some island were fed sweet potatoes by throwing the food into the sand. At first most of the monkeys ate the sweet potatoes, sand and all. But then one monkey decided to wash the sand off and then eat the sweet potato.

As the experiment progressed, more and more of the monkeys began to wash their sweet potatoes off before eating them. Finally, one monkey, the one called the hundredth monkey, washed off their sweet potato too.

Then all the remaining members of the colony broke and everyone began washing their potatoes before eating them.

It seems that when one extra person does anything in cooperation with others, it causes a breakthrough for the whole population. Gandhi said that what we do to create a better world may never be recognized by anyone. We may never have our names written in the history books, be interviewed on television, or win famous prizes and honors for what we do. But, he added, it is crucial that we do them. Otherwise they may not get done, and the world will be engulfed by one or more of the waves threatening it.

Each of us is the only one of us in the whole universe. Joe Wise says never in the history or in the future of the universe will there ever be another "us." That is how individual and unique we all are. We are the only ones who can contribute our talents for the human family, for the creation of the Solar Age. Once we have made our decision to go for broke, to refuse to accept the idea that we are powerless, then the rest of Fuller's critical paths seem to just spring out of the ground around us.

Once you have decided to act, then the second critical path is *education*. Fuller was once asked what one person can do. He quickly responded, find out what is not being done and do that. There is a historical movement going on all around us. The air is alive with information about people doing many great things. With a little seeking after your area of interest, you will quickly find the right place for your time and talents.

There are nine areas of education and activity. The first is the only real one, ourselves. Who we are and what we are doing makes the world the way that it is. The way that we live our everyday lives has an impact on the total reality of the planet. Our diets, our purchasing habits, our garbage are all a part of the total picture.

From there we move to our mates and dates. Next come our friends and relatives and then our work associates. After that, in order, are the city, county, state, "country,, continent, and the planet. There is not really a question of *what* to do, but *how* and *when* we are going to do it.

There is work to be done and multitudes of people and organizations waiting for you to do it. You may very well be the hundredth monkey that licks the one stamp and envelope that reaches the one person who does the correct thing to keep the planet alive. Or you may even be the person receiving that envelope!

The third path is the *creation of a global society*. In many regards this has already been done. Even though "countries" continue to act as if they are separate, they still recognize they have to deal with one another in some fashion. Science and technology have produced all kinds of global things: war, pollution, hunger, poverty, telecommunications, sports, business, and travel.

What is lacking is a true *economic* union. "Countries" have yet to be intertwined into a common system that will benefit us all. In the next chapter, we will discuss this union in greater detail through the coverage of Fuller's Global Grid Initiative.

After economic union is achieved, then the fourth critical path is easily completed. This is the *creation of a global nation* by the signing of a legal constitution. Most of the present "countries" began by joining together smaller states. A friend from Moscow showed me a coin made in North America in 1763. They asked me who was president then. I answered there was not even a United States in 1763! That was something dreamed up by guys like Jefferson and Washington. Now the idea is the same except it is us doing the dreaming and the "country" is the planet.

What has often driven political unions in the past is an outside threat to all of the people in all of the separate states. Their individual survival could only be gained by joining all of the states together to meet a common foe. The American colonies in 1776, really "countries" by their standards, joined together as Americans because they were being persecuted by the British.

There is a story about a person in the U.S. Marine Corps. The platoon was always having fights with another platoon on the base. However, when the two platoons were on leave in a nearby town, they were often confronted by members of another branch of the U.S. armed services.

Then they became Marines against the Navy, Army, or Air Force. And whenever any service person was confronted by a civilian, then they all joined together to be one against this enemy. And when the service people and the civilians came up against anyone from another "country," they were united as Americans.

Today the world is being confronted by the common dangers of a dying environment, by impoverishing military budgets, and the enslavement to joyless jobs. The solution to these problems is the same as for the "countries": to install a government, a democratic system of rule, to secure our rights to a safe life, liberty, and the pursuit of happiness.

Only by unified cooperation will we have any chance of a peaceful transition from our outdated Oil Age reality to the Solar Age reality. We need a government founded on the Declaration of Independence to safeguard ourselves at the *human* level.

In *Common Sense*, Thomas Paine described the function of government this way. He said, imagine yourself on a deserted island. He said the island could be a "country," or the world for that matter. On the island is a very large tree where the citizens carry out the business of running the island.

At first all of the citizens can meet under the tree and make their decisions. But as the population increases, not everyone will fit under the tree. Representatives are elected and they decide for the rest of the people what is going to be done. But for us the arrival of television and computers means we can *all* carry out the business of running *our* island, the earth.

In some cities today there is a means for a television viewer to respond to the show they are watching. Suppose there is a show on about cooking. The host prepares a meal and tells the viewers that if they want a copy of the recipe, to *vote* now. The viewers use the communication device in their homes and vote on getting a copy of the recipe. Those who wish to have a copy have their names brought up by the computer and the recipe is mailed out.

The same method is possible in making the decisions of government. Viewers watch the debate on the issues that interest them. The elected representatives' only job is to present all of the information. When the call for a vote is made, then the viewers from all over the world cast their ballot.

No longer will political reality be run by a small group of the elite who may or may not have our well-being in mind. Computers instantly tally the votes and then we deal with the outcome. This system is workable for any number of voters because the electronic speed of the computers can keep track of billions of such actions.

The bottom line is that all of the decisions must agree with the master law of the Declaration of Independence. The nature of politics is agreement, compromise, and lawmaking. There will be no utopia overnight, only its birth. In time, deciding local and global questions will be a truly democratic, peaceful process.

The biggest advantage of this system is the spreading of power to the people who are directly affected by the decisions being made. The outdated Oil Age idea of a central government calling *all* the shots is far too backward to meet the rapid and sudden changes brought on by the information of the Solar Age.

There are many groups today that want to be self-governing but are forced to join large "countries" or enter into a bloody revolution. With a global system of spreading power, each unit can be organized as they wish and then networked into the general community of the planet.

In fact, this system allows for *more* freedom of expression than does the outdated Oil Age ideas of "countries." These units can organize themselves into political units based upon common ground values. As members of a global nation, we can declare our backyard a "country" if we want. It is all part of the same nation, the earth.

People who eat the same kinds of food, speak the same language, go to the same church, or have the same kind of culture in dress, dance, music, and so on would probably get along. The outdated Oil Age idea that bigger is better makes for political unhappiness by trying to force an unnatural sameness on unique people.

And what fun the world would be! Going to so many different places where our common humanity is free to express itself in so many different ways would be like going to different planets. By recognizing our common humanity and ensuring its security by world law, we free ourselves and our children to be true individuals.

There are a number of global constitutions already in existence. The Constitution and Parliament Association in Lakewood, Colorado is seeking 10 million signatures to ratify its constitution for the world. The only thing lacking in pulling all of this off successfully is the demand from me and you for it to be done. We must declare ourselves free of the outdated Oil Age and bring forth our committed action for the creation of the Solar Age's possibilities and opportunities.

Common sense tells us there is only one "country" here, the world. Common sense tells us there is only one race here, the human race. Common sense tells us if not now, when? Common sense tells if not us, who?

CHAPTER FIVE

▼

KESSLER'S KWOTES

It is my firm conviction that once the psychological impediments are over come the solution of the real problems will not be a terribly difficult matter.

—Albert Einstein

We are getting all of the right technology for all of the wrong reasons.

—R. Buckminster Fuller

The Earth and myself are of one mind.

—Chief Joseph

I've been in this business for a long time, and I know it's a matter of persistence…I'd rather try something and fail than to look back ten years and say I wished I had.

—Harry Chapin

I have a dream.

—Martin Luther King, Jr.

You gain strength, courage and confidence by every experience in which you really stop to look fear in the face...you must do the thing you cannot do.

—Eleanor Roosevelt

Stop doubting your own love. Stop doubting and see yourself as love.

—Anonymous

CHAPTER FIVE

▼

WORLD PEACE AND THE GLOBAL GRID INITIATIVE

Whenever anyone discusses the idea of world peace, a very common reaction is that it is impossible. People love to cite all of the violence and disagreement aired so powerfully on television news shows. They say all of the conflicting governments, religions, and traditions make any such thinking foolish, utopian, or just plain crazy. And usually their comments are capped off with the ultimate excuse that there is nothing the individual can do anyway.

Then, in the middle all of this chatter, miracles happen. Great changes occur in what appears to be overnight. The Soviet Union undergoes a radical change in leadership and words like *glasnost* and *perestroika* pop into our vocabularies. The result is that a "country," the Soviet Union itself, ceases to exist. The Berlin Wall, which stood for nearly thirty years as an indestructible barrier to world peace, comes tumbling down. Two "countries" merge after 45 years of separation to form one Germany. These and countless other events around the world reveal the true reality in which we live.

Generally ignored by the media, which focuses on tragedies, millions of people just like us are working day in and day out for world peace. Then after decades of committed work and sacrifice, there bubble forth the Gandhis, Mother Teresas, Martin Luther Kings, and Nelson Mandelas. Each represents millions of other unknown, unsung heroes who are doing their part to secure our self-evident, divinely endowed, inalienable rights of life, liberty, and the pursuit of happiness.

And once again it is proven that what looked like overnight wonders are actually the result of years, maybe a lifetime, of nonstop work. The question naturally arises then, what if everyone, or a simple majority of people, put forth some positive effort? What kind of world would we have then? The answer is peace on Earth, individual wealth and freedom, and the dawn of a new reality for ourselves and our children.

Historically, one-third of people supports an idea of change, another third opposes it, and the remaining third is indifferent as long as their boat is not rocked too much. Einstein said that if 5 percent of the people worked for peace, peace will prevail. He based this on the 1 percent law in physics. 1 percent has an effect on the outcome of an event and 5 percent will determine its outcome in a predictable way.

Fuller referred to us as trimtabs. He said the rudder on an ocean liner has too much resistance from the water to turn the ship directly. The trimtab is a small device on the bottom of the rudder. When the pilot turns the trimtab, it turns the rudder, which turns the ship.

We are all part of the historical thirds. We are the 5 percent. We are all trimtabs. We are all part of the experiment to see if we will survive here much longer. We are all steering our spaceship planet by the actions we take or do not take. It is the individual, as Margaret Mead pointed out, that always changes things. True, it takes the synergetic effort of many, but first and last, we act alone.

Alvin Toffler brought out in *The Third Wave* that some generations are born to maintain a reality, which he called civilization. Other generations are born to create a new reality. With the information explosion of the twentieth century and the unprecedented global problems we are facing, we had better be a creating generation. The outdated Oil Age is on a collision course with extinction, and only we can steer our future to where we wish to go.

There are four stages that a reality goes through in its life cycle. The first is the *dream* stage. Our present outdated Oil Age began with the vision that the world is round and not flat. Eventually this new dream of reality replaces what came before it and people accept it as their own.

This introduces the second stage, the *affluent* stage. In this indefinite period of time, generations live and die within the opportunities offered by the new reality. These first two stages of the outdated Oil Age lasted from about 1400 to 1905.

Then comes the third stage, the *decadent* stage. Problems arise that the outdated reality cannot solve. The systems that had worked so well begin to break down. In fact, the reality becomes the problem. We call our outdated Oil Age breakdowns war, pollution, hunger, poverty, racism, sexism, and so on.

Once the reality has reached its decadent stage and begins to break down, there are two ways it can go. It can continue its present course and head straight into *demise*, which in our case translates into extinction. Or the reality is replaced by information that offers new possibilities and opportunities. It enters into a new dream. It follows a new vision.

Until the 1960s we seemed to be hell-bent for extinction. However, the world underwent a cultural revolution during that decade that shifted our thinking from the past. The seeds planted in those 10 years are now beginning to bear fruit as seen by the tremendous upheavals around the world.

The decade began with the orbiting of a human around the planet for the first time. The world's first global telecast occurred with the airing of the Beatles' *All You Need Is Love*. And in 1968 our picturing of the planet was changed forever with that photograph taken of the earth. Now it is time for our everyday traditions to catch up with what is real and no longer be chained to the outdated Oil Age ideas of the past.

James MacGregor Burns listed four levels of control in his Pulitzer Prize-winning book, *Leadership*. The first is *reward/punishment*, which is used by parents and dictators to keep children and dissenters in line. Then comes the second level, *peer group pressure*. In our outdated Oil Age this is called World War I and World War II.

The third level is *legal control*. This where our self-evident, divinely endowed, inalienable right to life, liberty, and the pursuit of happiness is made secure by law and not by the force of arms. The fourth, and highest, level is *self-control*. At this level the world is populated by humans, *energy beings of creativity*, who live in the reality of peace, love, prosperity, and individual freedom.

As a planet, we are on the verge of the third level of control. We are clumsily forging a Solar Age reality from the visions of Einstein and Fuller. The only question now is just how fast we want to have it. The answer lies in the committed action of each of us.

In the 1960s Fuller, aware of the new reality being born around him, created *World Game*™. It is a think tank to study the world's problems and resources to see what shows up as missing. He said if the military can have war games to see how to destroy the world, we can have World Game™ to make it a success.

He found out that the production and distribution of *electricity* lay at the heart of most problems. His studies revealed that when electricity shows up in an area, hunger disappears, population explosions stops, and longevity increases. He concluded that these and other problems can be solved by providing cheap, abundant sources of electricity.

Fuller also noted the increased construction of transmission lines since the end of World War II to connect local generators. These generators produce more power than can be used in their area. It was quickly discovered that it is cheaper to build connecting lines from these stations to other ones than to build a whole new station.

Gridded together, electricity soon becomes a product that is bought and sold upon demand. Most industrial "countries" are gridded together at the national level, and there are already over 50 connections between "countries."

Fuller combined this information with space-age technology that can transmit power over thousands of miles. This means that hookups between continents are possible. Therefore, he proposed in 1969 to build a *global energy grid* to supply the whole world with cheap, abundant electricity.

The major need now is for construction of a number of key connections to tie the existing grids into a foundation for a global network. The place where the first connection makes the most sense is at the Bering Strait. The United States and Russia are already gridded together at the national level, and they are separated by only 53 miles of water. A connection there means we can have a nonstop flow of power from one Atlantic seaboard to the other. It also opens up unlimited, clean power to Asia and Australia.

Another key connection is from North America to South America. There are great sources of power to be obtained from waterfalls in Central and South America. Generators, like those at Niagara Falls, can be installed to create huge amounts of electricity, without harming the beauty of the falls. This power is then available to uplift the quality of life for local people and to sell the excess on the world market for much-needed hard currency.

A third point of connection is between Europe and Africa. The solar potential of the Sahara and the waterfalls of sub-Saharan Africa are awesome. The Sahara is larger than the United States and is unused! The advantages of this connection are the same as for the Americas: a higher standard of living and a restored environment.

The importance of the grid cannot be overstated. It provides unlimited power for the immediate improvement of life for everyone: power to refrigerate medicines, to drive labor-enhancing machinery for irrigation and fresh drinking water; power to light, heat, and cool homes; power to cook food.

Fuller recognized that Einstein opened the door to a universe that is nothing but energy. Our fossil fuels are only the *stored* energy that hit our planet millions of years ago. The twentieth century has made technology possible to shift from getting energy out of these outdated sources to harvesting the energy directly as we *receive* it.

Fuller envisioned lining the seacoasts of the planet with tidal generators that create small amounts of power. This power is then fed into the grid to generate greater power. This one synergetic system provides enough power to meet our present needs for electricity, and we do not have to burn one lump of coal, or one drop of oil, one cubic liter of gas, or split one atom.

Once on-line, the grid will tie together the now remote renewable generation sites into a global, synergetic network. With one side of the planet always facing the sun, we have access to an unlimited, pollution-free power source. The desert areas of the planet can have environmentally friendly collectors to feed this abundant power into the grid. Add to this the other forces of tide, wind, and geothermal sources, and we will make fossil fuels and nuclear fuels truly that-FOSSILS.

The contribution to world peace is the biggest asset of the grid. We become buyers and sellers of one another's excess power. "Countries" do not bomb their customers. Fuller even saw kilowatts replacing money. The grid is also a peaceful, cooperative project that benefits everyone on Earth. It is then only a small step to make this intertwined economic community into a true nation by the adoption of a global constitution.

It has been said that a project has two main parts. The first is where a lot of effort must be put forth to realize a small amount of progress. This is where we are with the grid. After enough people have taken their go-for-broke, committed action, the project gets up enough steam and rolls along on its own power.

Then the project enters into the second phase where small amounts of effort produce great progress. All of the changes we witnessed in Europe since 1989 were the signs of attaining phase two, and walls literally came tumbling down. When enough of us direct our efforts to the grid, then we will see the exact same results. The grid will be turned on, and we will give birth to the Solar Age.

Have you ever seen trees broken by the weight of a heavy snowfall? When the storm begins, the first snowflake comes to rest upon the tree. Then another lands, and then another. More and more the tiny flakes quietly continue to pile up nonstop until the tree begins to bend. Eventually one additional snowflake softly lands, and the tree comes crashing to the ground.

We are creating the future now. How it turns out will be determined by each of us, by how we live our everyday lives, by what we do. More and more people are awakening to the reality of the Solar Age. More and more people are making their go-for-broke, committed actions count. Around the world the outdated Oil Age traditions are groaning and bending under the weight of people going for their dreams and visions.

CHAPTER SIX

▼

KESSLER'S KWOTES

I do think it essential that we should come forward with a positive program; a merely negative policy is unlikely to produce any practical results.

—Albert Einstein

Sometimes I think the world ought to go fishing.

—R. Buckminster Fuller

To believe what has not occurred in history will not occur at all is to argue disbelief in the dignity of (humans).

—Mohandas K. Gandhi

Every being, except humans, knows the purpose of life is to have a good time.

—Johann Wolfgang von Goethe

Life is either a daring adventure or nothing at all.

—Helen Keller

CHAPTER SIX

▼

THE SOLAR AGE

What does a reality based on the ideas of Einstein and Fuller have to offer us? It has an experience of life as different from our present reality as ours is from the Stone Age. It opens the door to unlimited wealth for everyone on Earth.

Fuller points out that in the past the problem was seen as taking wealth from the rich, usually through violence, and giving it to the poor. He says we now have the opportunity to raise everyone up to a level of wealth that no king has ever known. There is no one now alive, or has ever been alive, who has had the wealth promised by the Solar Age.

Instead of playing and replaying the dead scenes of "countries" and scarcity economics, the Solar Age offers us the choice of creating a dynamic, new future. Instead of putting our youngest and finest into Oil Age aircraft to shoot one another down as members of warring "countries," we can launch them together as crews of spacecraft to explore the stars.

The technology that has come out of the small space explorations we have done has already revolutionized life on Earth. With the resources of our planet diverted from "killingry" to the "livingry" of Solar Age technology, we harvest the abundance the real universe is waiting to give us. This technology, operating along with the environment, ends for all time hunger and war, and cleanses the environment.

The Solar Age offers us the opportunity to spend less time, eventually no time, on earning a living and more time, eventually all of our time on enjoying life. How much of the planet have you seen? Where would you like to go? What part of the world would you like to see, all expenses paid? The Solar Age is creating more leisure time. Currently it is called unemployment or early retirement. Within the structure of a global nation, our leisure time transforms into a lifelong, paid vacation.

As more and more of us are freed to explore our dreams and visions, the result is an explosion of inventions and discoveries. Already the advancements of the Solar Age are putting outdated Oil Age machines into museums. Imagine a planet where billions of free, healthy, well-fed, liberated minds are busily occupied with their pet projects.

Fuller said all of this and more is awaiting us once we get rid of the blood clots of separated "countries." They slow down or even stop the free flow of ideas, goods, and services. Once we leave this way of thinking behind, the healing of the Earth and the freeing of humanity can be done quite rapidly. Einstein said in 1946 that it would take less than ten years. Developments since then would make the time seem to be overnight.

This possibility of freeing us to pursue our dreams and visions is the most exciting aspect of the Solar Age. The end of the outdated Oil Age rat race means the rebirth of our childlike human spirit. After the flat world way of thinking was replaced by the round-world way of thinking, there was an explosion of creativity called the Renaissance.

From seemingly nowhere there appeared Michelangelo, Da Vinci, and Galileo. The Renaissance of the Solar Age will produce geniuses like them by the caseload. The flowering of art, science, athletics, and every other kind of human expression will be awesome.

There is an adjustment to unlimited free time. All of history has been a reality of having to work yourself to the bone just to survive. Our time is eaten away slaving at some job, paying the bills, and worrying about not falling behind. What leftover time we do have is absorbed by other tasks around the home and raising our families. Into all of this we squeeze in our dreams and visions—or give them up.

Once all of this is done away with by a superior Solar Age *way of thinking*, we are free to fill our days and nights with other things. As energy *beings of creativity*, our natural drive to do something fills this new free time easily. Look at children, especially those under age three. They have no problem eating up every waking moment with play and exploration. Each of us has unfulfilled, childhood dreams and visions to start us on our way. Once free from the drudgery of earning a living, they reawaken to fill our hearts again.

And what about when the frontier of the Solar Age has been passed? What will life be like when the Solar Age *is* the reality into which everyone is born?

In our history classes we will study war, hunger, poverty, and pollution like we now study the dinosaurs. Once these creatures ruled the earth for millions of years. Then quite suddenly they all went extinct. And like the asteroid that hit the planet and contributed to the dinosaurs' extinction, the Solar Age is roaring down on the outdated Oil Age.

The Solar Age means *peace* on Earth. Not just the absence of war, but a whole new era of opportunity. Eventually the people born into the Solar Age will outnumber those of us who are the fossils of the outdated Oil Age. They will grow up with a human, global identity and not ever engage in the insanity now making our world home an armed camp of hate and fear.

Earth, restored to its original purity, becomes a campus playground. New Adams and Eves come of age on an Edenlike planet. Rivers of pure drinking water flow into oceans untainted by Oil Age sludge. The air is washed clean of the gases now making it difficult to breathe and turning our rainwater to acid. The land once again becomes fertile and rid of poisonous chemicals polluting our foods and bodies.

Many people dismiss such statements as utopian idealism. *It is!* It is a vision of a world that works. The main difference between this idealism and those of the past is that *now it can be done*. In fact, to believe that we can continue as we are with the outdated ideas of the Oil Age is not only not realism, it is suicidal. The reality of the Solar Age based upon Einstein and Fuller is true realism, not flights of fantasy of the past.

For centuries people dreamed of flying through the air like the birds. In the first part of this century it became a choice with the invention of the airplane by Orville and Wilbur Wright. Eyewitnesses of the Kittyhawk flight rushed to a local newspaper office to report what they had seen. The editor replied that someone was pulling a hoax because a heavier-than-air machine had never been built, was impossible to build, and would never be built. Meanwhile, two unknown bicycle makers from Dayton, Ohio were quietly out on the dunes transforming reality.

All great periods of transformation are met with skepticism and resistance. Someone once said everything they let go of had claw marks on it. It is hard to let go of traditions that give us our personal identity. It is like killing off a part of ourselves. This is true and normal. But burst free of these straightjackets we must. It is time for us to be greater than what we have become, and to become what we are— citizens of the Universe.

The only thing standing between us and the freedoms of the Solar Age is our *own* skepticism and resistance. Overcoming that and doing the committed action needed are all there is to it. Starting with Fuller's global energy grid and the creation of a world government, the future awaits us and our children.

CHAPTER SEVEN

▼

KESSLER'S KWOTES

Education is that which remains if one has forgotten everything he has learned in school.

—Albert Einstein

(Young people) recognize that the world's resources belong to everyone, not to the nation that just happened to have had a dinosaur die in it

—R. Buckminster Fuller

The only tyrant I accept in this world is the still small voice within.

—Mohandas K. Gandhi

Pain in life is inevitable; suffering is optional.

—Kathleen Casey Theisen

Genius is one percent inspiration and ninety-nine percent perspiration.
—*Thomas Edison*

Service is the rent you pay for your spot on Earth.
—*Muhammed Ali*

A real friend is one who walks in when the rest of the world walks out.
—*Walter Winchell*

Great necessities call out great virtues.

—*Abigal Adams*

CHAPTER SEVEN

▼

CONCLUSION

The idea of a global nation is truly an idea whose time has come. Technology has reached every point on Earth through transportation and communication. And there is an urgency to unify our planet into one political, social, and economic nation. It arises from the common threats of pollution, nuclear weapons, world starvation, and the frustrated dreams and visions of us all.

Of all the twentieth century commonsense truths, the foremost is that there are no "countries." There are no little dotted lines that we have drawn on our maps and souls. By living in these make-believe straightjackets, we box up, if not abandon, our personal dreams and visions. We squander our time, energies, and resources to pay for meaningless military weapons with only one purpose: to kill every last one of us. Why are we condemning ourselves and our children to play and replay out the past?

Common sense tells us that the rest of the labels we use to describe ourselves are as artificial as "countries." Watch children under three and they will show our true reality. They will show a loving, playful *energy being of creativity.*

But some say children just have not learned about the real world yet. The truth is we have *forgotten* it by suffocating ourselves within the outdated traditions into which we were born and brainwashed. The fairy tale reality of "countries", race, age, money, and gender conceals our true reality as *energy beings of creativity* in an abundant universe. The result of this fairytale reality is that we judge everything at the level of appearance. But we are not appearances. We are energy. We are spirit.

The whole universe is made of the same stuff. The soil of the moon contains aluminum, magnesium, and iron. Our outdated scarcity ideas that there is not enough to go around evaporates before the commonsense reality of unending, recycling abundance. The real universe of Einstein and Fuller is waiting to make us all fabulously rich. It only makes common sense to create the political, social, and economic systems that can give us a new and prosperous future.

And that future begins with the creation of a constitution for a global nation. Common sense tells us that there is only one nation here: the world. Common sense tells us there is only one people here: the human family. There is no sense in continuing on the dead-end road of the past. This outdated tradition of separated "countries" goes against the basic order of nature that says everything is connected to everything else.

Buckminster Fuller said what made us a success on this planet was our ability to organize objects from our environment to solve a problem. From spears to spaceships, humans create what we need to survive and prosper. Now that we know *how* the universe works, we can design and create anything we can dream. In creating Design Science, Fuller said the experiment part of our existence is over. We have entered the creative phase of our existence.

All of the universe operates by a set of rules Fuller called *general operating principles*. The basic truth of these principles is that cooperation and networking are more productive than competition and separation. On the basis of these principles, he developed *synergetics*, the idea that things working together are more productive than working separately. In fact, the cooperation itself creates new opportunities and possibilities not available to competing things. That resulted in a wealth of inventions such as the geodesic dome, the Dymaxion house, the Dymaxion car, the octet truss, and many, many others.

From synergetics and World Game™, Fuller created the Global Grid Project to provide the planet with a peaceful, cooperative enterprise to uplift the standard of living of everyone. Most of the problems we are facing are rooted in the generation and distribution of electricity. The Global Grid Initiative offers abundant, clean energy to meet the problems now endangering life on our planet.

Our problems are solvable with existing technology, but our outdated *way of thinking* is standing in the way. Before we can use this technology, each of us has a personal crisis to overcome. We have a crisis of spirit. We each have a go-for-broke commitment to make in order to meet our challenges head-on and to do whatever it takes to be successful. And once we make our commitment, once we decide to create the Solar Age, once we decide to create a peaceful and prosperous future for ourselves and our children, then all of the necessary technology to do the job is here and ready to go.

Since 1945 more and more of the world's generators have been connected with others to form power grids. Excess electricity is bought and sold from one grid member to another. It is a simple matter now to connect these grids into one network and extend that throughout the whole planet. Less than one percent of the world's military budget can pay for it.

The first goal is to join the light and dark sides of the planet together with a connection across the Bering Strait. North America and Russia are nationally almost 100 percent gridded together already and are separated by only 53 miles of water. This one connection will form the global grid's foundation. From it the grid can be extended through Asia to Australia, from Europe to Africa, and from North to South America.

Now that Einstein has proven the universe is nothing but energy, we no longer need to look for outdated sources of power like fossil and nuclear fuels. They are only the stored energy that hit our planet long ago.

The grid allows us to retire these outdated Oil Age ideas of power. Now we can plug directly into one of the dynamos of the universe, our local star, the sun. Fuller calculated that if you added up all the energy from the fossil fuels used in one day, the sum equals only 1/4,000,000,000 of one percent of the energy we *receive* from the sun in one day. Energy need not be created, only harvested.

And this energy is present in the form of our environment. The combination of tidal, wind, geothermal, and solar energy form a synergetic blend to provide unlimited, free, clean power forever. The grid's removal of outdated fuels means the end of the greenhouse effect, environmental destruction, nuclear waste, and acid rain.

Fuller's World Game™ showed that when basic power is provided to an area, hunger disappears, the population explosion stops, and life expectancy increases. People have power to refrigerate medicines and food, to store grain, to run irrigation pumps, and to light, cool, and heat their homes.

A global nation, ruled by law, all but erases the need to sink wealth into the killingry of the military. Instead of globally wasting two million dollars a minute on weapons, we redirect this wealth to livingry technology to restore the world to a state of purity unseen for centuries.

Someone once said that if nothing changes, nothing changes. Many of us act as if the *world* must change and *we* can stay the same. If we, as individuals, do not change our beliefs and daily actions, none of us will live to enjoy the magnificent glory the Solar Age is offering. What we will see is the death of our planet from the results of our outdated Oil Age *way of thinking*. We are each now challenged to go beyond our personal frontiers.

The moment of transformation is instantaneous. It happens immediately, and we make our go-for-broke decision to do something. There are plenty of books, seminars, workshops, and organizations to inform us about what is being done and what needs to be done. The task takes courage and persistence, but the fate of every living thing on Earth hangs in the balance.

As was once said, if it is to be, it is up to me. We are the only ones who decide how and what we contribute. And our planet is in such a delicate condition that anywhere we look, there is something vital that needs attention. There are groups dedicated to the same issues that move you.

Remember Fuller's synergetics: Things working together are more productive than things working in competition. There are urgent problems in our lives, homes, neighborhoods, cities, counties, states, "countries", and on our planet that need our life, fortune, and sacred honor committed actions.

I coined the word *eracism* (AIR'-uh-cism) to refer to love of the earth as patriotism does for a "country." We all have a hometown, state, and "country." These ideas are okay for knowing where to send the mail. But the only true home we share is the planet, *our* Earth, and the universe itself.

We stand at the crossroads of success or extinction, and our individual actions determine the outcome. Millions of people around the world are doing wonderful things to make it a success. Like the unsung heroes that brought forth the changes of history, these present day heroes are bringing forth changes too. They are people like you and me, who see their responsibility and their opportunity to transform the world.

The global energy grid and a global nation offer us a firm foundation to enter the Solar Age. Our human family on this planet stands before a whole new era of peace and prosperity. Let's secure the future for our children, and ourselves, to blossom as the *energy beings of creativity* we are.

What are we waiting for?

APPENDIX I

DO UNTO OTHERS

The major creeds of the world have at the center of their moral teaching a simple statement which has come to be called the "Golden Rule." Considering the variety of beliefs, languages, and cultures represented by these faiths, it is remarkable that the *core teaching* is the same.

—Anonymous

CHRISTIANITY: Treat others as you would have them treat you; this sums up the law and the prophets. (Matthew 7:11)

JUDAISM: What is hateful to you, do not to your fellowman. That is the entire law; all the rest is commentary.(Talmud, Shabbat 3id)

ISLAM: No one of you is a believer unless he desires for his brother that which he desires for himself. (Sunnah)

BUDDHISM: Hurt not others in ways that you yourself would find hurtful. (Udana-Varga 5, 18)

HINDUISM: This is the sum of duty: do naught unto others which would cause you pain if done to you. (Mahabharata 5, 1517)

CONFUCIANISM: Is there one maxim which ought to be acted upon throughout one's life? Surely it is the maxim of loving-kindness: Do not unto others what you would not have them do unto you. (Analects 15,23)

APPENDIX II

*Global Energy Network Institute (GENI)
Source Document on R. Buckminster Fuller's
Global Grid Project*

*Peter Meisen, Director
Global Energy Network International(GENI)
World Trade Center of San Diego,9th floor
San Diego, CA 92101
619-595-0139
FAX 619-595-0403
Website—http://www.geni.org/
e-mail: geni@cerf.net*

Global Energy Network Institute

"The global grid
is the World Game™'s
highest priority objective"

—*R. Buckminster Fuller*

An opening statement:

This summary represents research developed over the past two years, and delves into the discussion of Ultra-High Voltage(UHV) power transmission. The context for this work comes from the proposal by Buckminster Fuller to connect existing regional energy grids into a world-wide grid system.

Since the scope of this investigation is so enormous, this report is in no way final, and is presented now to expand the research, educate and foster debate. Many questions remain unanswered, and many more have not been asked yet. Our desire is for the reader to explore [their] resource bank, and offer pertinent data and direction.

Peter Meisen
Director
Global Energy Network Institute (GENI)
…an educational initiative.

Introduction

"Humanity teeters on the threshold of the greatest revolution in history. If it's to pull the top down and it's

bloody, all lose. If it is a design science revolution to elevate the bottom and all others as well to unprecedentedly new heights, all will live to dare spontaneously to speak and live and love the truth, strange though it often may seem."

B. Fuller

When Buckminster Fuller was asked by a 12 year old boy, "How would you suggest solving international problems without violence?", he answered:

"I always try to solve problems by some artifact, some tool or invention that makes what people are doing obsolete, so that it makes this particular kind of problem no longer relevant. My answer would be to develop a world energy grid, an electric energy grid where everybody is on the same grid. All of a sudden there would be no problems anymore, no international troubles. Our new economic basis wouldn't be gold or dollars; it would be kilowatt hours."

A simple, yet elegant, and profound response.

The following discussion revolves around the technology of Ultra-High Voltage (UHV) power transmission. As with any engineering endeavor, there are many technical issues that could be presented. However, the approach in this summary will be more comprehensive, exploring many of the ramifications of power and societal development. The Global Energy Network Institute (GENI) proposal is definitely a complicated technical undertaking…but so was putting a man on the moon.

Surprisingly, the development of UHV power transmission systems affects many global issues: stemming population growth, ending hunger, environmental protection, international trade, political cooperation, and world peace. And we will discuss these in more detail.

The request to the reader is to wear the hat of a "world planner" as you read; and to imagine yourself an astronaut, circling the Earth. From this perspective, the one thing all astronauts agree is that no political boundaries can be seen from space. As a global planner, you must look beyond the immediate short term issues, and conclude society's needs over the next fifty and one hundred years.

The World Game™

Before we can address the specific proposal, a foundation must be laid; a context for the entire argument created. To do this, one must acknowledge Buckminster Fuller as the originator, and critical thinker of this proposal.

Buckminster Fuller has been called the Leonardo da Vinci of our time. He was a mathematician, cartographer, architect, inventor, author, poet; a visionary of extraordinary quality. Fuller is most well known for the geodesic dome. There are now over 300,000 domes around the world; one covers the South Pole research facility, they protect 100,000 radar installations, and are in thousands of playgrounds. Fuller died in 1983 at the age of 87.

One of his greatest gifts to humanity is the World Game™. A game that bypasses politics, human ignorance, prejudice and war, it is the opposite of war games, which are "played" by nations to develop strategies to win wars in the shortest time with the least casualties.

The purpose of the World Game™ is:

"To make the world work for 100% of humanity in the shortest possible time through spontaneous cooperation without ecological offense or the disadvantage of anyone."

Most every human, without exception, would agree this to be a worthy goal.

To best visualize our planet on a flat surface, Fuller developed a new world map projection called the Dymaxion™ map. It is the most accurate map with respect to the relative shapes and sizes of the continents. For example, the well known Mercator projection shows Greenland to be three times the size of Australia, and the exact opposite is true. If you trace the outline of the Dymaxion™ map, cut and fold along the triangular faces, you'll create the circular 20-sided polygon, called an icosahedron. From this you can see why the unfolded flat projection is so accurate.

On the Dymaxion™ map are placed 100 dots; each dot represents 1% of humanity or 50 million people; and each dot is placed in the most central location for that population base. A quick study reveals how crowded India and China are, compared to the rest of the world.

The second map also has 100 dots. As a world planner, what's important to recognize here is that the population is split 14% in the western hemisphere and 86% in the eastern hemisphere; and 90% live north of the equator while only 10% of humanity lives south of the equator.

In the World Game™, you input all the planet's resources, human needs, trends and technical know-how. Society and human needs are many: food, water, shelter, health care, education, communications, travel, economics, infra-structure like roads, sewers and energy. The goal of the World Game™ is to deliver resources so that everyone's standard of living can be improved to the "bare maximum". (We're all familiar with the notion of bare minimum—just enough to survive. Bare maximum is the upper resource target/capita so that everyone can fully realize their potential.) Since our focus in this summary is energy, our goal will be for everyone to receive a bare maximum number of kilowatt-hours per capita per year.

****

At this point, a couple of key statistics are important to dispel some myths:

Humanity's daily receipt of energy(solar only)= 4.15×10^{15}

Humanity's daily conversion of energy(all uses)= $.22 \times 10^{12}$

(Note the difference in scale between 10^{15} and 10^{12}.)

We receive thousands of times more energy than we could ever use or need. We use only a tiny fraction of what we receive.

"There is no energy shortage. There is no energy crisis. There is a crisis of ignorance."—B. Fuller

" The biggest danger in our present energy planning lies in not being imaginative enough to see the wide range of choices available."
—W. Peden

****

Note: The discussion about UHV power transmission does not involve all the arguments over the different types of energy generation: oil, gas, wood, nuclear, hydro, solar, wind, geothermal, tidal, etc. There are many strong debates published about renewable and non-renewable power generation sources. Since the Global Energy Grid proposal is about *transmitting* power, we won't enter into the generation debate here.

****

A Global Energy Grid

"The Global Energy Grid is the World Game™'s highest priority objective."

—*B. Fuller*

Delivering power everywhere by wire became the World Game™'s highest priority after studying human needs, and what constitutes a high standard of living.

"Throughout our work we found ourselves returning to one common denominator: Can you industrialize an area without electrical power? How can you take care of [people's] essential needs as to allow [themselves] to develop [their] unique metaphysical abilities? Whether we had researched food, communication, travel, housing, or economics, we always returned to electrical energy once we began to formulate any hypothesis about satisfying [human] needs. In order to enable people to be fed properly we found that they would first have to have a sufficiently high input of electrical energy to process, transport, and store food and dispose of wastes." —World Game™ lab

Electrical power is the common denominator that runs through every facet of a developed society. Since our focus is now electrical energy, and because power by wire is the fastest way to move energy, there are four fundamental things to know about electricity:

1. Electricity travels at the speed of light—186,000 miles/second. (The Earth' circumference is only 25,000 miles.) This means that the light you're reading by is being generated, transmitted and used at virtually the same instant.

2. Large amounts of power cannot be stored; it is generated and used. Generators are either producing power "on", or idle "off."

3. Power generators, especially fossil fuel and nuclear, are most efficient when run 24 hours/day- continuously.

4. However, the demand for power varies with the time of day. The demand at night is low when the lights are off and people are sleeping. The demand is high during the day when people and businesses are working.

Generators are successively turned on as more power is needed during daytime, and generators are cycled off as demand goes down in the evening. The cycle continues every day, for every city around the world, and utilities have calculated this use pattern for each hour of the day. Given that generation is most efficient when run 24 hours/day, this is not necessarily an efficient use of generators. In addition, excess power must always be generated in case of emergencies and for reliability of the power grid. If not sold, this excess power is a total loss to the utility since it provides no income, and can never be recouped.

UHV power transmission lines have solved the problem of wasted power for the utilities. By linking themselves with UHV lines, utilities can buy and sell power between themselves. If a utility can buy cheaper power than generating it itself, then a real win-win relationship is created. The buyer wins by getting cheaper power and not having to use/turn on a generator; and the seller wins by being able to sell the excess power for profit.

Thirty years ago the limit of efficient transmission was 350 miles. Then through technical breakthroughs by our space program (new metal, ceramics, etc.), the new effective distance became 1,500 miles. This means utilities could now span adjoining time zones, and begin to even out the peak and valley use patterns of the different time zones.

Over the last 25 years, power grids have become extensive and interconnected. There are large regional power grids in the

Soviet Union, Europe, Scandinavia, Mexico, and the western and eastern United States. These grids have expanded for purely economic reasons, but several other benefits have been derived (which we'll get to later).

Current research shows that UHV DC (direct current) transmission today has an effective distance of 4,000 miles! Although no such interconnection of this length exists, this now means we can begin to connect power grids between continents. This is where Fuller's proposal comes in, offering a dramatic expansion of currently feasible technologies that stand to benefit every human being on the planet.

Fuller recognized the possibilities of this technology thirty years ago. He proposed interconnecting the regional power grids into a world wide energy grid…connecting the progressive day and night halves of the planet into one Global Energy Grid.

By doing this, you at least double the available generation capacity for everyone, with a resulting reduction in cost (or to say it another way, an increase in everyone's standard of living). This would allow generators on the nighttime side (say the east) to continue running, and sell the power to the west for profit. And this power would be cheaper to buy for the west during the high demand daytime load. The situation reverses twelve hours later— or more exactly the system is dynamic based on the 24 times zones.

No new generators need be built, just the UHV lines to connect them. A massive win-win relationship. In corroboration, the United Nations Resources Committee forwarded the global grid proposal in 1971, but the discussion was killed by the politics of the day.

Some would argue, at this point, that this proposal would make us dependent on others for our power needs. We suggest, rather, that an *interdependence* is created that is mutually beneficial, and non-threatening.

There is plenty of precedent for linkages between countries, as 26 nations already have interconnections with neighboring countries.

Technical Feasibility: The State of the Art

It is important to understand that the Global Energy Grid proposal is not a Buck Rogers-Star Wars technology. As was mentioned, power grids continue to expand throughout Europe, the [former] Soviet Union, Mexico, Canada and the United States. An example is that 90% of the [former] USSR's power generation is currently interconnected, and the next 5 year plan commits to linking 100% of their generating capacity. What's especially exciting about the [former] Soviet geography is that their [former] nation spans 11 times zones, and can therefore can take full advantage of the demand pattern differences.

The international trade association of utility engineers, CIGRE (International Conferences of Large, High-Voltage Electric Systems), meets in Paris every two years. A recent conference unanimously agreed that greater and greater blocks of electric power will be transmitted over longer and longer distances throughout the world in the future. Continuing, they stated the value of interconnections turned out to be far greater than the estimates of savings than when they where originally planned.

Quoting from an article in "Electric Power and Light":
"Transmission ties with neighboring utilities
and interconnections between regional pools are
adding a new dimension to integrated electric
utility system operations. In addition to providing
bulk power backup during peak demand periods
and emergencies, transmission interconnections
are allowing more and more utilities dependent on
expensive oil and natural gas as boiler fuel to
turn to neighboring utilities with their over-abundant,
coal-fired and nuclear capacity to meet their base
load customer electricity requirements. The result:
economic benefits for all."[12]

Countries divided by a body of water can now be connected underwater with the technology of High-Voltage DC cables. A scheme between France and England is being upgraded to a 2000 megawatt capacity. (The original tie-line had a 160 MW capacity.)

The Electrical Power Research Institute published a book entitled *Electricity: Today's Technology, Tomorrow's Alternatives.* The following excerpt is from a section called "The Promise of HVDC":

"Where scarcity of land and concern with the appearance of power equipment favor the use of underground cables to feed electricity into urban areas, HVDC may be the system of choice…Opening up western coal fields far from the urban areas could mean the location of new coal-fired power plants far from those who consume the power …Another important role for DC lines is to connect existing AC systems. In many places it is virtually impossible to link neighboring systems because uncontrollable power instabilities could result …Links of DC can act as buffers. They control the power flow by converting AC to DC and then back to AC again. The DC link essentially de-couples the two AC systems, removing the need to attempt synchronization of their frequencies. These benefits, plus the fact DC transmission cuts in-transit power losses, suggest a bright future for HDVC."[13]

We have the technology, and the economics make sense. The barriers to expanding grids are bureaucratic and ideological.

Social Implications
Economical and Environmental

In the early 1970's, two AC lines and one DC line were built between Southern California and the Bonneville Power Administration on the Columbia River in Washington. In a recent report from the United States General Accounting Office to the Department of Energy, it states:

"With the completion of the intertie in 1970, the predominantly hydro-electric generating system of the Northwest was interconnected with the predominantly oil and gas-fired thermal generating system of California. This intertie also made Canadian power available through the Northwest into California.

Because of the different types of electric generation in the Pacific Northwest and California, both regions have benefited from the intertie. By the late 1970's, California had saved billions of dollars in revenue from the sale of surplus Northwest power. In addition, the nation as a whole has benefited from the transactions because as California predominantly purchases hydropower, it displaces oil and gas-fired generation, which lessens the nation's dependence on foreign countries for fuel sources."[14]

A recent report in "Spectrum," the engineer's magazine, is entitled "HVDC: Moving Lots of Power." It starts by saying that "moving from where it is plentiful to where it is needed may be more efficient than building oil-fired and nuclear plants locally."[15]

Both articles emphasize the massive economic win-win relationship for all parties; utilities, businesses and consumers; and stress the elimination of resultant wastes generated by thermal plants (nitrous and sulfur oxides) and radioactive wastes from nuclear plants.

Since peak demand power is usually generated by the most inefficient, expensive, and polluting generators during its brief on-time, and the peak demand period is when utilities will purchase cheaper power from a neighboring utility, the inadvertent result is a benefit to the environment.

And using the Pacific Intertie example; if billions are saved on a single 1000 mile interconnection, the savings potential of a Global Energy Grid are mind-boggling.

Hunger

In a developing society, nothing affects their standard of living quicker than the infusion of electricity. Whether for lights, refrigeration, irrigation or a radio, electricity begins to radically shift the amount of time spent on mundane tasks.

The enclosed maps and charts compare several population variables (taken from the United Nations Population Data Sheet), and energy statistics (from the United Nations Energy Data Sheet). The index used by the United Nations to determine whether hunger is a society-wide issue is the Infant Mortality Rate (IMR). The IMR is the annual number of deaths to infants under 1 year per 1,000 live births. If a country is below 50 IMR, hunger is considered to be a society-wide issue, if above 50 IMR, hunger persists.

If you compare kilowatt hours per capita per year with IMR, you discover that as energy becomes available to a developing society, the infant mortality rate drops. You'll readily see that energy rich countries are hunger-free, and energy poor countries are hunger prone.

Fuller predicted that once the Global Energy Grid was in place that hunger would end and industry would boom.16

Population

World population recently hit 5 billion people, and many world planners forecast massive problems as this growth continues.

First, it is known that the growth we are experiencing is mainly in the developing world, and that the modern world has basically a steady growth rate. The growth rate in the developed countries has most recently been attributed to longer life spans and immigration.

If you compare the kilowatt per person per year vs. birth rates you will see that as energy comes to the developing world, birth rates will decrease. Once a family can sustain itself, there is no need for the "insurance births" that create such large families in order to support elders in later life.

Trend studies that support these statements were done for every nation, and the results are shown. The trend lines from 1957-1977 show that as energy becomes available, birth rates drop in almost a one to one correlation.

Fuller said that the population explosion will cease when the Global Energy Grid is in place, and a bare maximum amount of power is available to everyone.17

Life Expectancy

The long life spans of modern society are a sure indication of a high standard of living. Again, if you plot kilowatt per person per year vs. life expectancy for all nations, you'll find that as energy becomes available, life expectancy increases.

****

Electric power is so pervasive in our society that we take it for granted, until there is a power failure…then everything stops. Electric power supports the entire structure in which we live. Bring this fundamental resource to a developing society and they too have the opportunity to flourish.

The Global Energy Grid proposal is a high-tech, capital intensive endeavor, and to suggest that this the immediate solution to the energy needs of a rural village would be absurd. What's needed now are small, localized power sources. But as the village develops, people will have heightened desires, and could eventually tap into the expanding network.

The Global Energy Grid plan is not an "either/or" proposal, but an "and/both" proposal. If attacked at both levels, the developing world could move into modern society by the turn of the century. [This document was written in the mid-1980's.—Kessler]

Technical Breakthroughs

Scientific advances in the electric utility industry continue to improve reliability, lower material costs, extend transmission, etc. This fits into a fundamental concept of Fuller's called "ephemeralization" or doing "more with less." It's the notion of getting more energy, more work, more efficiency out of less time and less resources.

A classic example of this is the 175,000 ton underwater communications cable between North America and Europe that is now surpassed in performance by a 1/4 ton satellite. A couple of examples in the power transmission field are: a new light-fired thyristor which converts AC to DC power is half the former size and will save millions over the life of a converter station, and an improved ceramic compound developed at Oak Ridge Labs that will help power grids absorb huge amounts of electricity.[18]

In the world arena, we already have two areas which function instantaneously: communications and the financial markets. The next should be electric energy exchange.

Paradoxically, many of the developments that benefit mankind come from the research on new weapons systems. Technical spin-offs have given society many labor saving devices. We suggest that our focus is often times misplaced, and should be on "livingry" technology, as opposed to "weaponry" technology. Fuller noted that most of the time we're doing "all the right research for all the wrong reasons."

Peace

The Global Energy Grid proposal affects many issues; perhaps one of the most basic is world peace. What is peace? Is it arms control, a cease fire, the absence of war? We suggest a much more dynamic, interrelated, mutually supportive relationship between nations. We all say we want peace, yet we spend billions of dollars in preparation for war.

In John Naisbitt's book *Megatrends* is a section entitled "World Peace through World Trade." He suggests that we should become economically interconnected with all nations, friend and foe. As we become consumers and suppliers of one another, we also become less likely to go to war with them. Using the example of Japan, just 40 years ago we were at war, and now we're so linked economically that we will work out any problems and never war again. Naisbitt suggests that we do the same with the [former] Soviet Union.[19]

A decade ago, Fuller had a friend in Canadian Prime Minister Pierre Trudeau. Trudeau was to meet with Soviet General Secretary Brezhnev. Fuller explained the Global Energy Grid proposal to Trudeau, who shared it with Brezhnev and his scientists. The response from those advisors was "desirable…feasible".[20]

The United States and the [former] Soviet Union currently spend over 2 billion dollars a day on their respective military machines that neither hopes will ever be used. There are lots of expectations around arms negotiations, but what if they did finally say "enough is enough." Millions of people would be thrown out of work because the "economic conversion" of the military-industrial complex was not well planned.

Well, the Global Energy Grid is a high-tech, whiz-bang challenge that scientists, engineers and computer professionals would love to sink their teeth into. Brain power, resources and capital could begin to roll over from both U.S. and [former] Soviet military budgets (weaponry) into the Global Energy Grid proposal (livingry). The Global Energy Grid is the *perfect high-tech global initiative that benefits everyone.*

The Cost

The cost of an Ultra-High Voltage line runs about one million dollars per mile (and can double in severe geography). If we want to build a line around the Earth on a great circle route (the Earth's circumference is 25,000 miles), the cost would be 25 billion dollars. A lot of money, but this is only 5% of the yearly US/USSR military budgets. Surely the money is available.

Many of the metal resources could come from the mothballed ships, old railroad cars and aircraft. After recycling, these metals could be made available for construction for pennies on the dollar since government dollars originally paid for much of these resources.

Both short and long term benefits far outweigh the cost of construction…and it would be a 24 hours a day, day in and day out, *breakthrough in trust and cooperation* between the world's superpowers.

Focused Project

Our discussion has been very comprehensive, and what many might call "futuristic." To bring the reader/astronaut back to Earth, let's focus on a specific project. What connection would make the most impact on the world arena?

The interconnection that fascinates everyone is the possibility of an HVDC line from the US/Canadian grid, across Alaska, the Bering Strait and Siberia, to the eastern (Russian) grid. This 5,000 mile span is one specific project which would galvanize world attention.

The Bering Strait...the 53 mile wide, 50 meters deep waterway between the Seward Peninsula of Alaska and the Chukchi Peninsula of Siberia. Why this project?

1. The international date line divides the Bering Strait, and is the key day/night link for the planet. It therefore has *massive* economic potential for both countries.

2. The technology already exists for underwater interties (English Channel between France and England) and the cost would be about two billion dollars.

3. Because it is the United States and the [former] Soviet Union, we would have a *new proposal* on the political platter; a synergistic project rather than the divisiveness that surrounds the dialogue of Nicaragua, Afghanistan, arms control, etc.

4. And, if the U.S. and [former] Soviets are talking about interconnections and the benefits, then every other nation around the world will be asking similar questions with neighbor nations.

The Bering Strait intertie should be the strongest link in the global chain...and be the metaphor for all the other connections around the world. The opportunity is for the superpowers to take a powerful lead by spanning 53 miles of water.

Summary

1. Fuller said the Global Energy Grid was the highest priority of the World Game.

2. Electric power was number one because it was discovered that for a society to develop, electricity was the common denominator of all the necessary infra-systems: food, shelter, travel, education, sewers, communications, health care, etc.

3. By connecting day and night halves of the planet, you at least double the available generating capacity of the planet, with the resultant lowered cost to everyone.

4. CIGRE, the utility experts, unanimously agree that greater and greater blocks of electric power will be transmitted over longer and longer distances throughout the world in the future.

5. 26 nations already have interconnections across their borders.

6. The [former] USSR has a full commitment to UHV technology, and 100% of their generating capacity is to be interconnected by 1990.

7. One of the fastest ways to world peace is through world trade. The Global Energy Grid links every nation into a win-win relationship which benefits every government, utility, business and consumer.

8. Tremendous economic benefits are derived through UHV interconnections. Since the Global Energy Grid is a high technology endeavor, it is a perfect transition project for the economic conversion of the United States and [former] Soviet military-industrial complexes.

9. Comparing the global trends of electric power vs. population statistics, Fuller predicts that as power becomes available to the developing world, infant mortality rates will drop, birth rates will drop, hunger will end and life expectancy will increase.

Conclusion

If the technology exists, and the economics make sense, why haven't we done it? Fuller said that we now have 160 admirals on "Spaceship Earth," all trying to steer the ship in different directions. And what they do is act as blood-clots on the free flow of resources and information. The barriers have been politics and bureaucracy.

What's been missing is an informed public that can influence political will. This is the purpose of GENI, to bring the issue up for discussion and debate.

A defined goal can cause all the current work in UHV to make sense in a grand scheme…and a defined goal can drive all future work with a new energy and purpose underlying each new interconnection.

"Muscle is nothing; mind is everything. But muscle is still in control of human affairs. In about 10 years, if we come out with muscle in control, we will have chosen oblivion; if we come out with mind in control, it's going to be utopia and eternity. Yes, we do have an option to make, but it is absolutely touch and go, a matter of the integrity of every human being from now on."[21]

B. Fuller

Bibliography/Footnotes

1. Gabel, Medard, *Energy, Earth, and Everyone,* Anchor Books, 1980

2. Brenneman, Richard, *Fuller's Earth*, St. Martin's Press, 1984

3. Hubbert, M.K., "The Energy Resources of Earth," *Scientific American*, Sept. 1971, and United Nations World Energy Data Sheet, 1978

4. op. cit. Gabel

5. Peden, W., "The Renewable Energy Handbook," *Energy Probe*, University of Toronto, Canada

6. Fuller, R. Buckminster, *Critical Path*, St. Martin's Press, 1981

7. Youngblood, Gene, "World Game Report," *La Free Press*, December 26,1969

8. Ibid.

9. Paris, Zini, Valtorta, Manzoni, Invernizzi, de Franco and Vain, "Present Limits to Very Long Distance Transmission Systems," CIGRE report, 1984 session

10. Central Intelligence Agency, *USSR Energy Atlas*, January 1985

11. Cassaza, John, "Interconnections Grow in Value", *Electrical World*, December 1984

12. Linicome, Robert, "Interconnections Provide New Operating Economics, as Well as Backup During Emergency, Peak Periods," *Electric Light and Power*, September 1984

13. Electric Power Research Institute, "Electricity: Today's Technologies, Tomorrow's Alternatives", 1987

14. General Accounting Office, U.S. Department of Commerce, National Technical Information Service, "Expanding the Pacific Northwest/Southwest Intertie- Benefits and Impediments," November 1983

15. Zorpette, Glenn, "HVDC: Wheeling Lots of Power," *Spectrum*, June 1985

16. Warshovsky, Fred, *Reader's Digest*, November 1969

17. op. cit. Fuller

18. Electric Light and Power, "Light Sensitive Thyristor Can Improve HV Systems," July 1983

19. Naisbitt, John, *Megatrends*, Warner Books, 1982

20. op.cit. Fuller

21. Snyder, Robert, *Buckminster Fuller: An Autobiographical Monologue Scenario*, St. John's Press, 1980

Appendix III

The Declaration of Independence

Section II

We hold these truths to be self-evident, that all (humans) are created equal, that they are endowed by their Creator with certain inalienable rights, that among these are life, liberty, and the pursuit of happiness. That to secure these rights, governments are instituted among [humans], deriving their just powers from the consent of the governed. That whenever any form of government becomes destructive of these ends, it is the right of the people to alter or abolish it, and to institute new government, laying its foundation on such principles, and organizing its powers in such form, as to them shall seem most likely to effect their safety and happiness. Prudence, indeed, will dictate that governments long established should not be changed for light and transient causes; and accordingly, all experience has shown, that mankind are more prone to suffer, while ills are sufferable, than to right themselves by abolishing the forms to which they are accustomed. But, when a long train of abuses and usurpations, pursuing invariably the same object, evinces a design to reduce them under despotism, it is their right, it is their duty, to throw off such government, and to provide new guards for their future security…

Appendix IV

World's One trillion dollar/year military budget

and

World Human Needs

$1 trillion a year

1. *35 seconds*—A. 1,000 classrooms for 30,000 children
          B. Save 4,000 tons of rice a year to feed 22,000 people
2. *12 minutes*—Provide 40,000 pharmacies
3. *2 1/2 hours*—Equals the entire World Hunger Organization's budget
4. *6 hours*—Oral re-hydration therapy to save 5 million kids a year
5. *10 hours*—Will provide contraception for the planet
6. *12 hours*—Eradicate malaria. Less to eradicate river blindness
7. *7 days*—Basic food to all the world's children
8. *12 days*—Safe drinking water for the planet
9. *3 weeks*—Primary health care for the world's children and immunization against the six most common diseases
10. *2 1/2 months*—Eradicate global hunger

0-595-22225-0

CPSIA information can be obtained
at www.ICGtesting.com
Printed in the USA
FSHW020329260220
67516FS